W9-CFL-615

Working with Young Children

Dr. Judy Herr
Professor, Early Childhood Education
School of Education
University of Wisconsin-Stout
Menomonie, Wisconsin

Publisher
The Goodheart-Willcox Company, Inc.
Tinley Park, Illinois
www.g-w.com

Cover photo: Penny Gentieu/Babystock/Jupiterimages

Introduction

This activity guide is designed for use with the text *Working with Young Children*. It will help you recall, review, and expand on the concepts presented in the text. It will also help you understand how to meet children's developmental needs as you teach and care for them.

The best way to use this activity guide is to begin by reading your assignment in the text. You will find that the activities in the activity guide correspond to the chapters in the text. Follow the instructions carefully at the beginning of each activity.

You will find a variety of activities in this guide. Some activities, such as true/false and matching activities, review text information. These can be used as study guides as you review in preparation for quizzes and tests. Do your best to complete these activities carefully and accurately. Try to complete as much of each activity as you can without referring to the text. Then compare the answers you have to the information in *Working with Young Children*. At that time you can also complete any questions you could not answer.

Other activities will ask for your ideas, opinions, evaluations, and conclusions that cannot be judged as right or wrong. The object of these activities is to encourage you to consider alternatives and evaluate situations thoughtfully. The text will be a useful reference in completing these activities.

The activities in this guide have been designed to be both interesting and fun to do. This activity guide will help you apply what you have learned as you work with children now and in the future.

Contents

Part 1
The Children and You

1 You: Working with Young Children 9
- A. Truths About Early Childhood
- B. Comparing Teaching to Other Careers
- C. Pleasures and Problems in Teaching
- D. Characteristics for Working with Children

2 Types of Early Childhood Programs 15
- A. Early Childhood Fill-In
- B. Types of Programs
- C. Choosing a Program
- D. Evaluating Early Childhood Programs

3 Observing Children: A Tool for Assessment 21
- A. Check Your Understanding
- B. Assessment Tools Summary
- C. Interpreting the Data
- D. Designing an Assessment Tool

4 Child Development Principles and Theories 27
- A. Understanding Development
- B. Erikson's Psychosocial Theory
- C. Dialing for Answers to Piaget's Theory
- D. Applying Multiple Intelligence Theory
- E. Check Your Theory IQ

5 Understanding Children from Birth to Age Two 33
- A. Types of Development
- B. Reflexes
- C. Development Fill-In
- D. Encouraging Development

6 Understanding Two- and Three-Year-Olds 37
- A. Development of Two-Year-Olds
- B. Studying Two-Year-Olds
- C. Development of Three-Year-Olds
- D. Studying Three-Year-Olds
- E. Self-Help Skills
- F. Language Skills

7 Understanding Four- and Five-Year-Olds 45
- A. The Truth About Preschoolers
- B. Reading and Math Fun
- C. Handling Emotions
- D. Developing Activities

8 Middle Childhood **51**
  A. Understanding Middle Childhood Terms
  B. Check Your Gender IQ
  C. Health Dilemmas
  D. Testing Mental Operations
  E. Beliefs About Middle Childhood

Part 2
Creating a Safe and Healthful Environment

9 Preparing the Environment **57**
  A. Meeting the Goals of a Well-Planned Space
  B. Responses to Color
  C. Activity Areas

10 Selecting Toys, Equipment, and Educational Materials **61**
  A. Toys Meeting Goals
  B. Age-Appropriate Equipment
  C. Actions to Take
  D. Comparing Prices

11 Promoting Children's Safety **67**
  A. Safety Procedures
  B. Fire Safety Evaluation
  C. Understanding Child Abuse

12 Planning Nutritious Meals and Snacks **71**
  A. Nutrients and Their Functions
  B. Nutrition Crossword
  C. MyPyramid
  D. Identifying the Sources

13 Guiding Children's Health **75**
  A. Health Match
  B. Communicable Diseases
  C. First Aid Kit Scramble
  D. Burns

Part 3
Guiding Children

14 Developing Guidance Skills **79**
  A. Direct and Indirect Guidance
  B. Positive Guidance
  C. Putting Effective Guidance into Practice
  D. Guidance Techniques

15 Guidance Challenges..83
    A. Guidance Match
    B. Guidance Tips
    C. Family Stressors Affect Guidance
    D. Dialing for Answers

16 Establishing Classroom Limits................................87
    A. Stating the Positive
    B. Limit Pyramid
    C. Know the Limits
    D. Setting Limits

17 Handling Daily Routines..91
    A. Your Style of Managing Daily Routines
    B. Planning a Daily Schedule
    C. Managing Conflicts

Part 4
Learning Experiences for Children

18 The Curriculum..95
    A. Dogs Web
    B. Learning Activities Related to a Theme on Dogs
    C. Behaviors
    D. Curriculum Building
    E. A Sample Lesson

19 Guiding Art, Blockbuilding, and Sensory Experiences 101
    A. Stages of Artwork
    B. Characteristics of Children's Art
    C. Sources of Free Art Materials
    D. Tips for Buying Art Supplies
    E. Rating Play Dough

20 Guiding Storytelling Experiences................................107
    A. Storytelling
    B. Choosing Books for Children
    C. Story Comparisons
    D. Evaluate Your Storytelling Technique

21 Guiding Play and Puppetry Experiences 111
    A. Playtime Match
    B. Encouraging Socio-Dramatic Play
    C. Design a Puppet
    D. Writing Puppet Stories

22 Guiding Manuscript Writing Experiences 117
    A. Practice Your Writing
    B. Manuscript Writing

23 Guiding Math Experiences 119
   A. Math Match
   B. Color, Shape, and Counting Concepts
   C. Teaching Space, Size, Volume, and Time
   D. Using Recipes to Teach Math Concepts

24 Guiding Science Experiences 125
   A. Science Overview
   B. Forming Open-Ended Questions
   C. Pet Care
   D. Methods of Teaching Science

25 Guiding Social Studies Experiences 131
   A. Social Studies Activities
   B. Using a Theme in Planning
   C. Know Your Resources

26 Guiding Food and Nutrition Experiences 135
   A. Teaching Nutrition
   B. Collecting Recipes
   C. Setting the Table

27 Guiding Music and Movement Experiences 139
   A. Musical Truths
   B. Rhythm Instruments
   C. Fingerplays
   D. Teaching Movement

28 Guiding Field Trip Experiences 143
   A. Community Field Trips
   B. Planning the Trip
   C. Before and After the Field Trip
   D. Completing the Trip

Part 5
Other People You Will Meet

29 Programs for Infants and Toddlers 147
   A. Caregiver Traits
   B. Environment Needs
   C. Toys for Development
   D. Child Care Procedures

30 Programs for School-Age Children 153
   A. Quality School-Age Programs
   B. My Ideal Environment
   C. Design a Survey
   D. Games for Fostering Development

31 Guiding Children with Special Needs 157
    A. Special Needs Match
    B. Special Communication Needs
    C. Physical and Health Disorders
    D. Helping Children Who Have Special Needs
    E. The Child Who Is Gifted

32 Involving Parents and Families 163
    A. Getting Family Involved
    B. Family Letters
    C. Family Discussion Groups
    D. Teacher Hotline

33 A Career for You in Early Childhood Education 169
    A. Assessing Your Abilities
    B. Know How to Job Hunt
    C. A Job Application
    D. Balancing Multiple Roles

Extra Lesson Plan Forms 175

Characteristics for Working with Children

Activity D

Chapter 1

Name _____

Date _____ Period _____

People who enjoy working with young children tend to have certain characteristics in common. Many of these characteristics are listed below. For each of the characteristics, rate yourself as (*S*) strong, (*A*) average, or (*W*) weak. Then have a family member or friend rate you on the same set of characteristics using the form on the following page.

_____	Active	_____	Humorous
_____	Affectionate	_____	Intelligent
_____	Alert	_____	Kind
_____	Ambitious	_____	Levelheaded
_____	Artistic	_____	Likable
_____	Broad-minded	_____	Nurturing
_____	Calm	_____	Organized
_____	Capable	_____	Patient
_____	Careful	_____	Practical
_____	Competent	_____	Realistic
_____	Considerate	_____	Resourceful
_____	Cooperative	_____	Responsible
_____	Creative	_____	Self-controlled
_____	Dependable	_____	Sensible
_____	Eager	_____	Serious
_____	Efficient	_____	Sincere
_____	Energetic	_____	Stable
_____	Enthusiastic	_____	Thorough
_____	Firm	_____	Tolerant
_____	Flexible	_____	Understanding
_____	Friendly	_____	Warm
_____	Healthy	_____	Well-groomed
_____	Honest	_____	Wholesome

Write in additional characteristics that you feel should describe someone who works with young children. Also rate yourself in these areas.

_____ _____

_____ _____

_____ _____

_____ _____

_____ _____

_____ _____

(Continued)

In the space below, have a family member or friend rate you (S) strong, (A) average, or (W) weak for each characteristic.

_____	Active	_____	Humorous
_____	Affectionate	_____	Intelligent
_____	Alert	_____	Kind
_____	Ambitious	_____	Levelheaded
_____	Artistic	_____	Likable
_____	Broad-minded	_____	Nurturing
_____	Calm	_____	Organized
_____	Capable	_____	Patient
_____	Careful	_____	Practical
_____	Competent	_____	Realistic
_____	Considerate	_____	Resourceful
_____	Cooperative	_____	Responsible
_____	Creative	_____	Self-controlled
_____	Dependable	_____	Sensible
_____	Eager	_____	Serious
_____	Efficient	_____	Sincere
_____	Energetic	_____	Stable
_____	Enthusiastic	_____	Thorough
_____	Firm	_____	Tolerant
_____	Flexible	_____	Understanding
_____	Friendly	_____	Warm
_____	Healthy	_____	Well-groomed
_____	Honest	_____	Wholesome

How would the characteristics in which you are strong benefit you in a career working with young children?

_____

_____

_____

_____

_____

What actions can you take to strengthen the areas in which you are weak?

_____

_____

_____

_____

_____

_____

Evaluating Early Childhood Programs

Activity D

Chapter 2

Name _____

Date _____ Period_____

Pretend you are a parent looking for an early childhood program for your child. Visit two centers and evaluate them by checking the appropriate answers to the questions listed below. Then summarize your overall impressions of each program. Tell which one you would choose for your child and why.

Name of center #1: _____

Name of center #2: _____

Questions to Ask	Center #1		Center #2	
	Yes	**No**	**Yes**	**No**
1. Is the center accredited by the National Academy of Early Childhood Programs?				
2. Do the children appear to be happy, active, and secure?				
3. Are all staff members educationally qualified?				
4. Do staff members attend in-service training, professional meetings, and conferences on a regular basis?				
5. Are staff meetings conducted regularly to plan and evaluate program activities?				
6. Do staff members observe, assess, and record each child's developmental progress?				
7. Does the curriculum support the children's individual rates of development?				
8. Do the staff and the curriculum celebrate diversity?				
9. Is the indoor and outdoor environment large enough to support a variety of activities?				
10. Is the environment inviting, warm, and stimulating?				
11. Is equipment provided to meet all four areas of development: social, emotional, cognitive, and physical?				
12. Are safe and sanitary conditions maintained within the building and on the playground?				
13. Are teacher-child interactions positive?				
14. Are teachers using developmentally appropriate teaching strategies?				
15. Are parents welcome to observe and participate?				
16. Is sufficient equipment available for the number of children attending?				
17. Does the climate in the center "feel" positive?				
18. Do teachers meet with families regularly to discuss the child's needs, interests, and abilities?				

(Continued)

Types of Early Childhood Programs **19**

Overall impressions of center #1:_____

_____

_____

_____

_____

Overall impressions of center #2:_____

_____

_____

_____

_____

Which center would you choose? Why?_____

_____

_____

_____

_____

_____

_____

Observing Children: A Tool for Assessment

Check Your Understanding

Name _____

Date _____ Period_____

Read the following statements related to assessment. Circle *T* if the statement is true or *F* if the statement is false.

T   F   1. Observation is one of the newest methods of learning about children.

T   F   2. Assessment is the process of observing, recording, and documenting children's growth and behavior over time.

T   F   3. Evaluation is the process of reviewing the information and finding value in it.

T   F   4. Assessment helps keep the teacher and curriculum responsive to the needs of children.

T   F   5. A child's strengths and weaknesses can be identified through the assessment process.

T   F   6. A single assessment is an exact assessment of ability or performance.

T   F   7. Developmental milestones are characteristic behaviors considered normal for children in specific age groups.

T   F   8. Formal assessment is often used by early childhood teachers.

T   F   9. Teachers prefer to use only one method for gathering information about the children.

T   F   10. Anecdotal records are the simplest form of direct observation.

T   F   11. Anecdotal records should include generalizations about the motives, attitudes, and feelings of the children.

T   F   12. Observations should always be factual and unbiased.

T   F   13. An interpretation attempts to explain observed behavior and give it meaning.

T   F   14. Interpretations may be influenced by feelings, values, and attitudes.

T   F   15. An anecdotal record requires no special setting or time frame.

T   F   16. Checklists may be developed to survey one child or a group of children.

T   F   17. Using a participation chart, teachers sometimes find that children's activity preferences do not match their needs.

T   F   18. Rating scales require you to make a judgment about behavior.

T   F   19. A child's random scribbles on paper are *not* needed for assessment purposes.

T   F   20. A portfolio can show the child's growth and development over time.

Assessment Tools Summary

Name _____

Date _____ Period_____

For each of the assessment tools listed, give possible advantages and disadvantages to their use. Then give an instance when this tool could effectively be used. Use your text to complete the chart as much as possible. Use other references or give your own opinion in order to complete the remaining portions of this chart.

Anecdotal Records		
Advantages:	Disadvantages:	Use:

Checklists		
Advantages:	Disadvantages:	Use:

(Continued)

Participation Chart

Advantages:	Disadvantages:	Use:

Rating Scale

Advantages:	Disadvantages:	Use:

Interpreting the Data

Name _____

Date _____ Period_____

Read the incident recorded on the anecdotal record shown in Figure 3-6 of your text. Then try your hand at interpreting the data by answering the questions below. Compare your interpretation with a classmate's and answer the remaining questions.

Your interpretation:

1. Why did Carrie hit and push Tony? _____

   _____

2. What might have been her motive?_____

   _____

3. Could someone or something have caused Carrie to act this way? _____

   _____

4. Why did Carrie smile as Tony left? _____

   _____

5. Why did Tony respond as he did when he was hit and shoved? _____

   _____

6. What might have been his motive for shrugging and walking away?_____

   _____

7. Could someone or something have caused Tony to act this way? _____

   _____

Comparing interpretations:

Since no two people interpret facts in the same way, read the interpretation of this incident written by one of your classmates.

1. How did your classmate's interpretation differ from yours? _____

   _____

   _____

   _____

2. What explanation can you give for this difference? _____

   _____

   _____

   _____

3. What conclusions can you draw from this comparison? _____

   _____

   _____

   _____

Designing an Assessment Tool

Activity D

Chapter 3

Name _____

Date _____ Period_____

Teachers often create their own assessment tools to meet their specific classroom needs. Design a simple checklist in the space provided below. Use the developmental milestones information in Appendix B of your text to make your checklist. Also refer to the samples in your text. Write the behaviors to be assessed in the column on the left. Then use your checklist to assess a child.

Age of child for which this checklist is designed: _____

Category of skill(s) being assessed (fine-motor, gross-motor, self-help skills, etc.): _____

	Yes	No

4 Child Development Principles and Theories

Understanding Development

Activity A

Chapter 4

Name _____

Date _____ Period_____

Complete the following sentences by writing the correct words in the blanks.

cephalocaudal

cognitive

development

fine-motor

gross-motor

infants

maturation

neurons

physical

preschoolers

proximodistal

social-emotional

synapses

toddler

windows of opportunity

_____ 1. From birth to one year, children are called ____.

_____ 2. Development tends to proceed from the head downward according to the ____ principle.

_____ 3. Specialized nerve cells in the brain are called ____.

_____ 4. Key times for brain synapses to link easily and efficiently are called ____ .

_____ 5. ____ development involves the interrelation between relationships with others and expression of feelings.

_____ 6. ____ development involves using the small muscles of the hands and fingers.

_____ 7. The processes learned to gain knowledge is called ____ development.

_____ 8. Running, skipping, jumping, and climbing fall into the category of ____ development.

_____ 9. Development proceeds from the center of the body outward according to the ____ principle.

_____ 10. ____ refers to the sequence of biological changes in children.

_____ 11. The growth or change that occurs in children is called ____.

_____ 12. Children ages from three to six years of age are called ____.

_____ 13. Children from age one up to three years of age are called ____ .

_____ 14. Changes in bone thickness, vision, hearing, muscle, size, and weight are all part of ____ development.

_____ 15. Links or connections between neurons are called ____.

Erikson's Psychosocial Theory

Name _____

Date _____ **Period**_____

Write a brief description of the first four stages of Erikson's psychosocial theory listed below.

1. Trust versus mistrust:_____

   _____

   _____

   _____

   _____

   _____

   _____

2. Autonomy versus shame and doubt: _____

   _____

   _____

   _____

   _____

   _____

   _____

3. Initiative versus guilt: _____

   _____

   _____

   _____

   _____

   _____

   _____

4. Industry versus inferiority:_____

   _____

   _____

   _____

   _____

   _____

   _____

Dialing for Answers to Piaget's Theory

Activity C

Chapter 4

Name _____

Date _____ Period _____

In the following exercise, the numbers below the blanks represent letters on the telephone dial. Use the clues and numbers to complete the following statements relating to guidance challenges.

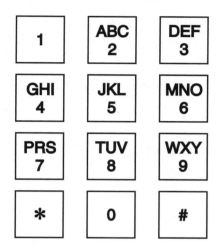

1. Piaget's theory of development focuses on predictable _ _ _ _ _ _ _ _ _ stages.
   2 6 4 6 4 8 4 8 3

2. His theory explained _ _ _ _ _ _ operations.
   6 3 6 8 2 5

3. _ _ _ _ _ _ _ _ are mental representations or concepts.
   7 2 4 3 6 2 8 2

4. The process of taking in new information and adding it to what the child already knows is called
   _ _ _ _ _ _ _ _ _ _ _ _.
   2 7 7 4 6 4 5 2 8 4 6 6

5. _ _ _ _ _ _ _ _ _ _ _ _ _ is adjusting what is already known to fit the new
   2 2 2 6 6 6 6 3 2 8 4 6 6
   information.

6. The first stage of development is called the _ _ _ _ _ _ _ _ _ _ _ _ stage and occurs
   between birth and two years of age.   7 3 6 7 6 7 4 6 6 8 6 7

7. During the preoperational stage of development, children are very _ _ _ _ _ _ _ _ _ _ _,
   assuming that others see the world as they do.   3 4 6 2 3 6 8 7 4 2

8. During the concrete operations stage, children develop the ability to _ _ _ _ _ systematically.
   8 4 4 6 5

9. Problem solving and _ _ _ _ _ _ _ _ _ are developed during the fourth state, formal
   operations.   7 3 2 7 6 6 4 6 4

Applying Multiple Intelligence Theory

Name _____

Date _____ Period _____

Match the following needs of children with their intelligence type.

_____ 1. Nature walks, gardening, and rock collections.

_____ 2. Manipulatives for measuring, matching, and counting.

_____ 3. Sharing of experiences, group activities, books focusing on emotions.

_____ 4. Role-plays, drama, creative movement, and hands-on activities.

_____ 5. Puzzles, blocks, and visual aids.

_____ 6. Rhythm instruments, singing, and music.

_____ 7. Storybooks, writing tools, paper, and discussions.

_____ 8. Classroom examples of emotions, areas to be alone, and self-paced projects.

A. bodily-kinesthetic
B. interpersonal
C. intrapersonal
D. logical-mathematical
E. musical-rhythmic
F. naturalistic
G. verbal-linguistic
H. visual-spatial

9. What type of intelligence do you believe is your strongest? Why? _____

_____

_____

_____

_____

_____

_____

_____

_____

_____

_____

_____

_____

_____

_____

_____

_____

_____

_____

_____

_____

_____

_____

Check Your Theory IQ

Name _____

Date _____ Period_____

Read the following statements. Circle a *T* if the statement is true or *F* if the statement is false.

T   F   1. Developmental theories provide insights into how children grow and learn.

T   F   2. The theories provided by Erikson, Piaget, and Vygotsky can be useful decision-making tools.

T   F   3. Erikson proposed a theory of multiple intelligences.

T   F   4. According to Erikson, during the first eighteen months children learn to trust or mistrust their environment.

T   F   5. According to Erikson, children who are provided unrealistic goals and expectations can develop feelings of incompetence.

T   F   6. Piaget believed that learning was *not* limited by stage or maturation.

T   F   7. As children receive new information, they are constantly creating, modifying, organizing, and reorganizing schemata.

T   F   8. During the sensorimotor stage, infants use all their senses to explore and learn.

T   F   9. Piaget's fourth stage, formal operations, occurs between seven and eleven years of age.

T   F   10. Piaget and Vygotsky believed that children build knowledge through experiences.

T   F   11. Vygotsky believed children learn through exploration with hands-on activities.

T   F   12. Vygotsky's theory includes eight stages.

T   F   13. Vygotsky believed that language is an important tool for thought and plays a key role in cognitive development.

T   F   14. One of Vygotsky's most important contributions was the zone of proximal development.

T   F   15. The term that Vygotsky used for providing assistance was *private speech*.

T   F   16. Howard Gardner's theory has helped teachers rethink how they work with young children.

T   F   17. Gardner believes intelligence is a result of complex interactions between children's heredity and experiences.

T   F   18. Gardner's theory of intelligence emphasizes that there are two types of intelligence.

T   F   19. Musical intelligence involves the ability to recognize musical patterns.

T   F   20. Logical-mathematical intelligence is the ability to use logic and reason to solve problems.

T   F   21. Young children with verbal-linguistic intelligence learn best by talking, reading, and writing.

T   F   22. People with intrapersonal intelligence display excellent communication and social skills.

T   F   23. Naturalistic intelligence allows people to use their vision to develop mental images.

T   F   24. Children with naturalistic intelligence process knowledge through sensation.

T   F   25. The brain affects all aspects of growth and development.

Self-Help Skills

Name _____

Date _____ Period_____

Read the following list of self-help skills. Write the word *two* beside each skill that is usually mastered by a two-year-old. Write the word *three* beside each skill that is usually mastered by a three-year-old.

_____ 1. Opens snaps and zippers.

_____ 2. Gets through the night without wetting.

_____ 3. Works buckles.

_____ 4. Puts on shoes that do not tie.

_____ 5. Begins to cooperate in dressing.

_____ 6. Pours liquid from a small pitcher.

_____ 7. Removes socks, shoes, and pants.

_____ 8. Washes and dries face and hands.

_____ 9. Closes snaps.

_____ 10. Uses knife for spreading.

_____ 11. Pulls on simple garments.

_____ 12. Starts using the toilet when reminded.

_____ 13. Turns faucet on and off.

_____ 14. Has almost full control over toilet routines.

_____ 15. Unbuttons large buttons.

_____ 16. Seldom has bowel accidents.

_____ 17. Understands pronouns *you* and *they*.

_____ 18. Understands words such as *up*, *top*, and *apart*.

_____ 19. Stands with both feet on a balance beam.

_____ 20. Begins to understand the difference between the past and the present tense.

_____ 21. Scribbles.

_____ 22. Builds a tower of six to seven blocks.

_____ 23. Constructs four- or five-word sentences.

_____ 24. Begins to use questions, especially *why* and *when*.

Language Skills

Name _____

Date _____ Period_____

Read the following list of language skills. Determine whether each is a language comprehension skill or an expressive language skill. Place a *C* in front of skills that are language comprehension. Place an *E* in front of skills that are expressive language skills.

_____ 1. Combines two or more words such as "Boy hit."

_____ 2. Understands and answers routine questions such as "What is your name?"

_____ 3. Uses prepositions in speech.

_____ 4. Follows three-part instruction.

_____ 5. Points to six body parts on self or doll.

_____ 6. Uses three-word sentences such as "You go home."

_____ 7. Uses plurals, such as "I want more cookies."

_____ 8. Uses negative terms such as "Mommy don't go."

_____ 9. Gives "just two" on request.

_____ 10. Understands the pronouns *you* and *they*.

_____ 11. Uses possessives such as "Mommy's coat."

_____ 12. Understands *smaller*.

_____ 13. Understands *larger*.

_____ 14. Provides appropriate answers for *how* questions.

_____ 15. Joins two sentences with a conjunction.

_____ 16. Uses adjectives, such as *pretty*.

 **Middle Childhood**

Understanding Middle Childhood Terms

Name _____

Date _____ Period_____

Match the following terms and definitions by placing the correct letters in the corresponding blanks.

_____ 1. Span of years between age 6 and 12.

_____ 2. Ability to see objects in a distance more easily than those that are close by.

_____ 3. Ability to see close objects more clearly than those at a distance.

_____ 4. Using logic but basing it on what has been seen or experienced.

_____ 5. Condition of having excessive body fat.

_____ 6. Technique children often use to remember information.

_____ 7. Manipulation of ideas based on logic rather than perception.

_____ 8. Ability to arrange items in increasing or decreasing order based on volume, size, or weight.

_____ 9. Principle that change in position or shape of substances does not change the quantity.

_____ 10. Ability to group items by common attributes.

_____ 11. Process where people define themselves in terms of qualities, skills, and attributes they see in others.

_____ 12. Belief that you are a worthwhile person.

_____ 13. Ability to understand the feelings of others.

_____ 14. Being aware of others' distress and wanting to help them.

_____ 15. The understanding and use of accepted rules of conduct when interacting with others.

_____ 16. The process of acquiring the standards of behavior considered acceptable by society.

A. moral development
B. farsighted
C. operation
D. classification
E. self-esteem
F. middle childhood
G. obesity
H. rehearsal
I. social comparison
J. empathy
K. nearsighted
L. seriation
M. conservation
N. morality
O. compassion
P. concrete operations

Check Your Gender IQ

Name _____

Date _____ Period_____

The text describes many differences in physical development and social behavior between boys and girls during the school-age years. Read the following statements. In the blank before each statement, write *G* if the statement generally describes girls and *B* if the statement generally describes boys. Then try to observe school-age children during a school recess period and answer the questions at the end of this activity.

_____ 1. Taller at the beginning of this stage.

_____ 2. Tend to occupy space closer to the school building.

_____ 3. Are more open than secretive in their relationships.

_____ 4. Interact in pairs or small groups.

_____ 5. Best at skills requiring balance, flexibility, or rhythm.

_____ 6. Reach 80 percent of adult height by the end of middle childhood.

_____ 7. Play involves more taking turns and cooperating with others.

_____ 8. Experience a growth spurt at age 12.

_____ 9. Have more physical strength.

_____ 10. Prefer jumping rope and doing tricks on the jungle gym.

_____ 11. Tend to control large fixed spaces at school that are used for team sports.

_____ 12. Weigh more by 12 years of age.

_____ 13. Experience a growth spurt at age 10.

_____ 14. Prefer competitive sports.

Observe a large group of school-age children of the same age during a school recess period. Look for the gender differences listed above. Then answer the questions below.

1. Which of the above characteristics about boys were you able to observe? _____

_____

_____

_____

2. Which of the above characteristics about girls were you able to observe? _____

_____

_____

_____

3. It is important that early childhood teachers do not reinforce gender-role stereotypes. However, gender differences do exist among school-age children. How do you feel a teacher should respond to this dilemma? _____

_____

_____

_____

_____

Health Dilemmas

Name _____

Date _____ Period _____

The situations below describe challenges you might face in handling health-related situations in the classroom. Break into small groups. Read each dilemma and discuss possible approaches to the situations. Write your group's best suggestions in the spaces provided.

1. You notice that Antwann, a seven-year-old, holds books four or five inches in front of his face. What might be his problem? What action should you take?

_____

_____

_____

_____

_____

_____

_____

_____

2. Amparo's behavior is frustrating you. He seems to ignore most suggestions. After listening to a story, his responses to questions are inaccurate. What action should you take?

_____

_____

_____

_____

_____

_____

_____

_____

3. Rhonda is an obese child. At lunch and during snack time, she takes more food than needed. As her teacher, what can you do to help Rhonda with her weight problem? How would you suggest working with Rhonda's parents?

_____

_____

_____

_____

_____

_____

_____

_____

Testing Mental Operations

Name _____

Date _____ Period_____

Children learn the concepts of conservation, seriation, and classification during the middle years. Design your own activities to test these concepts with a child between the ages of six and ten. After testing the child, record their responses below.

Age of child tested: _____

Conservation

Describe how you plan to test the child's understanding of the concept of conservation:_____
_____
_____
_____

What supplies will you need? _____
_____

What results do you expect that will show the child understands conservation?_____
_____
_____

What were the results of your test with the child? _____
_____
_____
_____

Seriation

Describe how you plan to test the child's understanding of the concept of seriation: _____
_____
_____
_____

What supplies will you need? _____
_____

What results do you expect that will show the child understands seriation? _____
_____
_____

What were the results of your test with the child? _____
_____
_____
_____

(Continued)

Classification

Describe how you plan to test the child's understanding of the concept of classification:_____

_____

_____

_____

What supplies will you need? _____

_____

What results do you expect that will show the child understands classification? _____

_____

_____

What were the results of your test with the child? _____

_____

_____

_____

Beliefs About Middle Childhood

Name _____

Date _____ Period_____

Read each sentence and circle the word choice that best describes your beliefs. Then explain your answer in the space provided.

1. I believe friendships take on a **lesser/greater** importance in middle childhood than before.

   Reason: _____

   _____

   _____

   _____

2. I believe teachers **can/cannot** play an important role in building a school-age child's self-esteem.

   Reason: _____

   _____

   _____

   _____

3. I believe children **should be/should not be** encouraged to participate in team sports and competition during middle school.

   Reason: _____

   _____

   _____

   _____

4. I believe playing games that involve rules **is/is not** important to a school-age child's development.

   Reason: _____

   _____

   _____

   _____

5. I believe teachers **should/should not** encourage school-age children to make social comparisons.

   Reason: _____

   _____

   _____

   _____

Preparing the Environment

Meeting the Goals of a Well-Planned Space

Activity A

Chapter 9

Name _____

Date _____ Period_____

Pretend you have been hired as the director of a new child care center. You have been asked to provide input into the design of the physical space. For each of the goals for a well-planned space listed below, give two examples of how you would meet that goal in designing the physical space.

Goal 1: To provide a physically safe environment for the children

_____

_____

Goal 2: To provide children with areas that promote cognitive, emotional, social, and physical growth

_____

_____

Goal 3: To provide an abundance of materials so children can make choices

_____

_____

Goal 4: To provide adults with a space that is easy to supervise

_____

_____

Goal 5: To provide space that is pleasing to the eye for both adults and children

_____

_____

Goal 6: To provide easy access to materials when needed so children are able to direct themselves

_____

_____

Goal 7: To provide a space with high activity and low stress where children can work and play comfortably

_____

_____

Responses to Color

Name _____

Date _____ Period_____

Read the name of each color listed. In the space provided, record your responses to each color. Then ask a preschool child to share his or her thoughts about each color. Record the child's responses. Answer the questions below the chart to note similarities and differences in the responses.

Color	My Thoughts	A Preschool Child's Thoughts
Red		
Blue		
Green		
Yellow		
Purple		
Pink		
Black		
Brown		

What similarities and differences did you find in the responses? _____

_____

_____

_____

_____

What might be some reasons for the differences?_____

_____

_____

_____

_____

Activity Areas

Name _____

Date _____ Period_____

List ten basic activity areas found in most classrooms. Name their functions and describe where each should be placed in the classroom.

1. _____
   _____
   _____
   _____

2. _____
   _____
   _____
   _____

3. _____
   _____
   _____
   _____

4. _____
   _____
   _____
   _____

5. _____
   _____
   _____
   _____

6. _____
   _____
   _____
   _____

7. _____
   _____
   _____
   _____

8. _____
   _____
   _____
   _____

(Continued)

9. _____
_____
_____
_____

10. _____
_____
_____
_____

Planning the outdoor play area is just as important as planning the indoor classroom areas. Answer the following questions about outdoor play areas.

11. List three guidelines for the best use of playground space.

_____
_____
_____
_____

12. What are nine other items to consider when planning an outdoor playground?

_____
_____
_____
_____
_____
_____
_____
_____
_____

 # Selecting Toys, Equipment, and Educational Materials

Toys Meeting Goals

Name _____

Date _____ Period_____

Listed below are two program goals for a group of three-year-olds. Read the goals and available toys and equipment. Then list additional toys and equipment that are needed to help meet the program goals.

Program Goals	Available Toys and Equipment	Toys and Equipment Needed
Goal A: To encourage language development.	*Books*	
Goal B: To encourage fine-motor development.	*Puzzles*	

Think of two or more possible program goals for a group of three-year-olds. List the program goals and toys that could help meet those goals.

Program Goals	Toys and Equipment Needed
Goal A:	
Goal B:	

Age-Appropriate Equipment

Name _____

Date _____ Period_____

Not all toys and equipment are appropriate for children of all ages. While some toys are suitable for infants, other toys are only appropriate for older children. Match the toys and equipment listed below with the age of the youngest children who should use them. Refer to Chart 10-9 in the text if necessary.

_____ 1. Activity gym.

_____ 2. Roller skates.

_____ 3. Cloth books.

_____ 4. Wooden telephone.

_____ 5. Tricycle.

_____ 6. Doll bed.

_____ 7. Play dough.

_____ 8. Small jungle gym.

_____ 9. Blunt scissors.

_____ 10. Pull toys.

_____ 11. Large wooden threading beads.

_____ 12. Giant dominoes.

_____ 13. Hard books.

_____ 14. Stacking and nesting toys.

_____ 15. Finger paints.

_____ 16. Walking board.

_____ 17. Scooter.

_____ 18. Coaster wagon.

_____ 19. Doll carriage.

_____ 20. Simple climber and slide.

_____ 21. Rattles.

_____ 22. Interlocking blocks.

_____ 23. Peg Boards.

_____ 24. Magnets and sand molds.

_____ 25. Sewing machine.

A. six-month to one-year-old

B. one-year-old

C. two-year-old

D. three-year-old

E. four-year-old

F. five-year-old

Actions to Take

Name _____

Date _____ Period _____

List an action you could take to improve the safety and performance of the toys and equipment listed below. Some items may need to be discarded.

Condition or Toy to Improve	Action to Take
1. Chipped paint	
2. Worn varnish	
3. Loose nuts	
4. Rusty equipment	
5. Squeaky bicycle wheels	
6. Broken plastic toy	
7. Play iron with cord and plug	

(Continued)

Condition or Toy to Improve	Action to Take
8. Toy gun	
9. War game	
10. Pull toy with small beads inside	
11. Swing seat with open S-ring	
12. Stuffed animal with button eyes	
13. Balloons	
14. Wooden swing seat	
15. Exposed screws and bolts	

Comparing Prices

Name _____

Date _____ Period_____

Find the price charged for each of the following items by three different sources. For instance, check prices using Web sites, catalogs, stores, and co-ops. You might also try to check prices of secondhand equipment. Record each price and the source of your information in the space provided. Also record any other notes you want to remember about that source.

Easel

Vendor 1:	Vendor 2:	Vendor 3:
Price (including any shipping costs):	Price (including any shipping costs):	Price (including any shipping costs):
Other important notes:	Other important notes:	Other important notes:

Sensory Table

Vendor 1:	Vendor 2:	Vendor 3:
Price (including any shipping costs):	Price (including any shipping costs):	Price (including any shipping costs):
Other important notes:	Other important notes:	Other important notes:

Tricycle

Vendor 1:	Vendor 2:	Vendor 3:
Price (including any shipping costs):	Price (including any shipping costs):	Price (including any shipping costs):
Other important notes:	Other important notes:	Other important notes:

(Continued)

Bookshelf

Vendor 1:	Vendor 2:	Vendor 3:
Price (including any shipping costs):	Price (including any shipping costs):	Price (including any shipping costs):
Other important notes:	Other important notes:	Other important notes:

Autoharp®

Vendor 1:	Vendor 2:	Vendor 3:
Price (including any shipping costs):	Price (including any shipping costs):	Price (including any shipping costs):
Other important notes:	Other important notes:	Other important notes:

12 Cans Tempera Paint

Vendor 1:	Vendor 2:	Vendor 3:
Price (including any shipping costs):	Price (including any shipping costs):	Price (including any shipping costs):
Other important notes:	Other important notes:	Other important notes:

Talk to people at two centers to learn whether the price quotations you received were realistic and whether a center could afford to pay those prices. Also ask for tips on how to obtain necessary equipment at the lowest possible cost. Record what you learn from these discussions.

_____

_____

_____

_____

_____

_____

Promoting Children's Safety

Safety Procedures

Name _____

Date _____ Period_____

Choose terms from the following list to correctly fill in the blanks in the statements related to safety.

child abuse	fire drills	limits	self-control
dangers	fire extinguishers	physical	spills
electrical	food	protection education	walk
environment	glass	rubber gaskets	windows
evacuation	helmets	seat belts	

_____ 1. Constantly be alert to potential _____, or unsafe situations.

_____ 2. The staff is responsible for planning a safe _____ for the children.

_____ 3. Planning safety _____ will help you meet the safety goal.

_____ 4. Post _____ procedures to use in various emergencies.

_____ 5. Immediately report suspected cases of _____ to the appropriate community agency.

_____ 6. Schedule an in-service on how to use _____ before the opening of the center.

_____ 7. Center vans and buses should have _____ in them to protect children.

_____ 8. Include _____ in the curriculum to teach children how to handle possible sexual advances from adults.

_____ 9. Child care centers are responsible for providing proper _____ storage.

_____ 10. Require staff to obtain an approved _____ exam before working with children.

_____ 11. Children who lack _____ and are hazardous to themselves and others should be removed from the classroom.

_____ 12. _____ outlets must be covered.

_____ 13. Remind children to _____ indoors rather than running.

_____ 14. Wipe up _____ right away.

_____ 15. Beware of stuffed toys that may have button or _____ eyes.

_____ 16. Schedule _____ on a regular basis such as once a month to practice evacuating the building.

_____ 17. Keep _____ closed at all times unless gates or sturdy screens are in place.

_____ 18. Children should wear _____ when riding bikes.

_____ 19. Doors should have _____ to prevent finger pinching.

Fire Safety Evaluation

Name _____

Date _____ Period_____

Visit an early childhood center. Use the checklist below to evaluate fire safety practices at the center. Read each statement and place a check mark in the appropriate column. Then answer the questions that follow.

Fire Safety Checklist	Yes	No
1. Exit passageways and exits are free from furniture and equipment.		
2. Locks on bathroom doors and toilet stalls can be opened easily from the outside by center staff.		
3. Protective covers are on all electrical outlets.		
4. Permanent wiring is used instead of lengthy extension cords.		
5. Each wall outlet contains no more than two electrical appliances.		
6. A fire evacuation plan is posted.		
7. Fire drills are conducted at least monthly, some of which are unannounced.		
8. Flammable, combustible, and other dangerous materials are marked and stored in areas accessible only to staff.		
9. Children are restricted to floors with grade level exits (no stairs).		
10. The basement door is kept closed.		
11. There is no storage under stairs.		
12. Fire extinguishers are in place and checked regularly.		
13. Smoke alarms and fire alarms are checked at least once a month.		
14. Matches are kept out of the reach of children.		
15. Toys, chairs, tables, and other equipment are made of flame-retardant materials.		
16. Carpets and rugs are treated with a flame-retardant material.		

1. How would you rate this center's fire safety practices?

	Poor		Good		Excellent
	1	2	3	4	5

2. Explain your answer. _____

_____

_____

3. Would you add any additional items to the checklist above? Why or why not? _____

_____

_____

4. Why do you think it is important to find and correct fire safety hazards in a center?_____

_____

_____

Understanding Child Abuse

Name _____

Date _____ Period_____

Using the information in the text, other reference materials, and your own opinions, respond to the following:

1. List and describe the four types of child abuse._____

   _____

   _____

   _____

   _____

   _____

   _____

   _____

   _____

   _____

   _____

   _____

   _____

2. Research an agency that helps prevent child abuse and/or works with people in child abuse situations. What support services are offered for families, and how are child abuse situations handled? How is a child abuse case reported? Record what you learn. _____

   _____

   _____

   _____

   _____

   _____

   _____

   _____

   _____

   _____

   _____

   _____

   _____

   _____

   _____

(Continued)

3. List and describe several characteristics that many child abusers have in common. _____

_____

_____

_____

_____

_____

_____

_____

_____

_____

4. What current social problems do you think contribute to today's problem of child abuse? _____

_____

_____

_____

_____

_____

_____

_____

_____

_____

_____

_____

5. What do you think teachers can do to help protect children from child abuse? _____

_____

_____

_____

_____

_____

_____

_____

_____

_____

_____

_____

Planning Nutritious Meals and Snacks

Nutrients and Their Functions

Name _____

Date _____ Period_____

Match the following terms and identifying phrases.

_____ 1. Build and repair tissues.

_____ 2. Supplies energy and carries fat-soluble vitamins.

_____ 3. Helps prevent night blindness.

_____ 4. Combines with proteins to make hemoglobin.

_____ 5. Helps cells use other nutrients.

_____ 6. Aids in blood clotting.

_____ 7. Promotes normal appetite and digestion.

_____ 8. Helps build bones and teeth; helps muscles and nerves function properly.

_____ 9. Helps transport nutrients and waste.

_____ 10. Helps regulate many body processes; helps build strong bones and teeth.

_____ 11. Provide bulk in the form of cellulose (needed for good digestion).

_____ 12. Helps keep skin, tongue, and lips healthy.

_____ 13. Helps body fight infection.

_____ 14. Acts as antioxidant.

_____ 15. Helps keep adult bones healthy.

A. calcium
B. carbohydrates
C. fat
D. iron
E. niacin
F. phosphorus
G. proteins
H. riboflavin
I. thiamin
J. vitamin A
K. vitamin C
L. vitamin D
M. vitamin E
N. vitamin K
O. water

Nutrition Crossword

Name _____

Date _____ Period_____

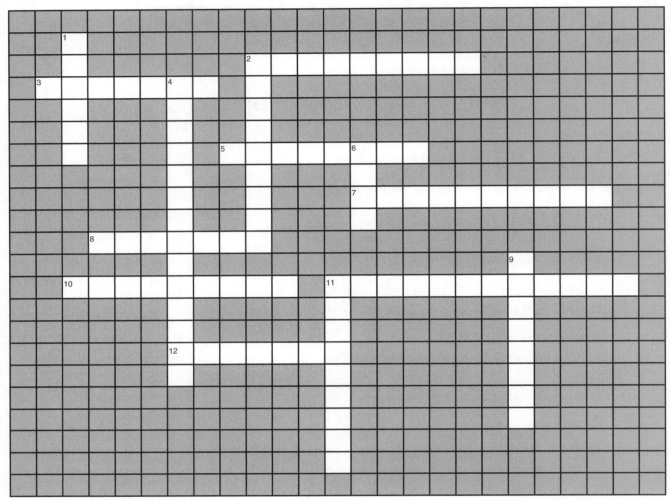

Across

2. Chemical substances needed for growth and maintenance of health and found in foods are called _____.

3. The most important nutrient provided by the milk group is _____.

5. Citrus fruits are rich sources of _____.

7. Taking in more food than the body needs to function properly is called _____.

8. The most important nutrient supplied by the meat and beans group is _____.

10. Many milk products have been _____ to include vitamins A and D.

11. _____ is a lack of proper nutrients in the diet.

12. _____ is a condition that can lead to health problems such as hypertension and diabetes during adulthood.

Down

1. A child's diet should include six ounce-equivalents of _____ daily.

2. The science of food and how the body uses it is called _____.

4. Not eating enough food to keep a healthful body weight and activity level is called _____.

6. The main sources of the mineral _____ are meat and meat alternates.

9. Deep yellow and dark green vegetables are rich sources of _____.

11. _____ is a set of online tools to help plan nutritious diets to fit individual needs.

MyPyramid

Name _____

Date _____ Period_____

A variety of food items are listed below. Place each of these items under the correct food group in MyPyramid.

cottage cheese apples   cheese   pea pods

collard greens   waffles   meatballs   crackers

kidney beans   granola   peanut butter yogurt

chow mein noodles broccoli   cheese fondue dates

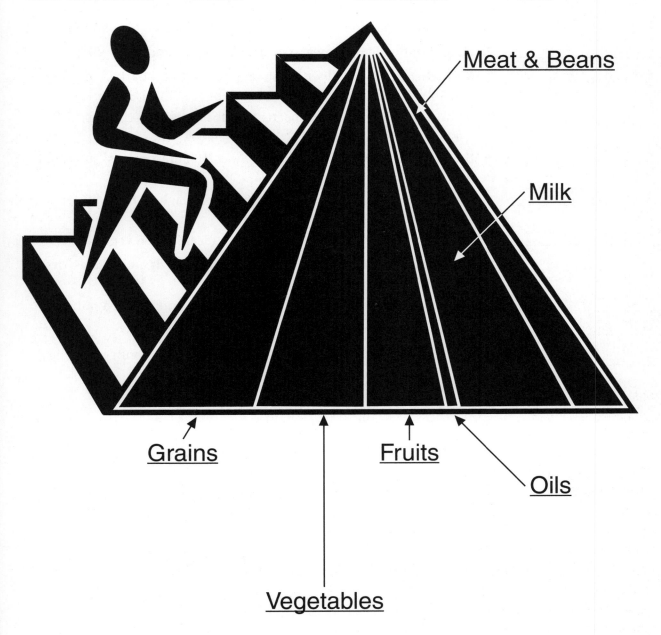

Identifying the Sources

Name _____

Date _____ Period_____

For each group of sources listed, fill in the blank with the name of the nutrient provided. Use each nutrient listed only once.

carbohydrates	fats	niacin
proteins	riboflavin	thiamin
vitamin A	vitamin C	vitamin D
vitamin E	vitamin K	

_____ 1. Egg yolk, organ meats, cauliflower, and leafy green vegetables.

_____ 2. Peanut butter, lentils, meat, poultry, fish, eggs, and dairy products.

_____ 3. Milk, cheese, yogurt, liver, meat, fish, poultry, and dark green leafy vegetables.

_____ 4. Breads, cereals, corn, peas, beans, potatoes, pasta, rice, fruits, vegetables, honey, sugar, jam, jelly, molasses.

_____ 5. Butter, cheese, cream, nuts, olives, chocolate, lunchmeats, and salad oil.

_____ 6. Dark green and yellow fruits and vegetables, whole milk, butter, cream, fortified margarine, and cheeses.

_____ 7. Whole grain cereals, liver, eggs, fats, and leafy green vegetables.

_____ 8. Pork, other meats, enriched or whole-grain breads and cereals, dried beans, pork, and fish.

_____ 9. Sunshine, tuna, sardines, fish liver oils, liver, and fortified milk.

_____ 10. Tomatoes, cantaloupe, broccoli, and citrus fruits.

_____ 11. Dried beans, peas, whole-grain cereals, fish, milk, poultry, and meat.

Guiding Children's Health

Health Match

Name _____

Date _____ Period_____

Match the following terms and definitions.

_____ 1. An injury caused by heat, radiation, or chemical agents.

_____ 2. A break in the skin.

_____ 3. A disease that results from a virus, breaks down the immune system, and, over time, can be fatal.

_____ 4. A scrape that damages a portion of the skin.

_____ 5. Condition in which a person has periodic seizures.

_____ 6. A disease caused by a viral infection of the nervous system and brain and commonly spread through animal bites.

_____ 7. Damage to the surface of the skin or body tissue.

_____ 8. Illnesses that can be passed to other people.

_____ 9. Small bugs that live on the hair and scalp and lay eggs called nits.

_____ 10. Can occur as a result of an extremely allergic reaction.

_____ 11. A reaction of the body to a substance in the environment.

_____ 12. An injury to the tissue directly under the skin's surface.

_____ 13. Disease in which the body cannot properly control the level of sugar in the blood.

_____ 14. The treatment of injuries and illnesses, including those that are life threatening.

_____ 15. An illness caused by eating food that contains harmful bacteria, toxins, parasites, or viruses.

_____ 16. Virus that breaks down the immune system and, over time, can lead to a more advanced disease.

_____ 17. A course of action that controls future decisions.

_____ 18. The process of eliminating all germs from surfaces.

_____ 19. The process of removing dirt or soil and a small amount of bacteria.

_____ 20. Designed to protect staff from accidental exposure to bloodborne pathogens.

A. abrasion
B. AIDS
C. allergy
D. anaphylactic shock
E. burn
F. closed wound
G. communicable diseases
H. diabetes
I. disinfecting
J. epilepsy
K. first aid
L. foodborne illness
M. head lice
N. HIV
O. open wound
P. policy
Q. rabies
R. sanitizing
S. universal sanitary control practices
T. wound

Communicable Diseases

Name _____

Date _____ Period_____

List the symptoms and incubation periods for the communicable diseases listed below. Refer to Figure 13-5 in the text.

Disease	Symptoms	Incubation Period
Chicken pox		
Conjunctivitis		
Hepatitis A		
Influenza		
Mumps		
Lice		
Ringworm		
Rubella		
Scabies		
Streptococcal infections		

First Aid Kit Scramble

Activity C

Chapter 13

Name _____

Date _____ Period_____

Unscramble the letters below to reveal items that belong in a child care center's first aid kit. Write the name of each item in the blank that follows it.

1. rstfi dia aanulm _____

2. elirste srift ida ssdsergni _____

3. rtsewzee _____

4. sssrocis _____

5. yfeats sinp _____

6. eic cakp _____

7. zeagu aasegnbd_____

8. isevehad etap _____

9. ttheeemmorr _____

10. aatintcbreila nisk rclenea _____

11. eeecgmnry acedilm bemnrsu _____

12. ynoirhorosedct mraec _____

13. rosabbtne ttoonc llsab _____

14. oohllca peiws _____

15. abdeilopss nnoooprsu eglosv _____

16. elbasopsid reppa ssseuti _____

17. tfgsialhhl _____

18. tnocot sbwas _____

19. kbnlaet _____

20. leptomeru lyjel _____

Burns

Name _____

Date _____ Period_____

Match the following descriptions to the types of burns described by placing the correct letter in the corresponding blank. Letters will be used more than once.

_____ 1. The least severe burns.

_____ 2. Destroy nerve endings in the skin.

_____ 3. Require immediate medical attention.

_____ 4. Common signs include mild discoloration or redness.

_____ 5. Can quickly become third-degree burns if infection arises.

_____ 6. An ambulance should be called immediately.

_____ 7. Healing is normally rapid.

_____ 8. Are likely to swell a great deal over a period of several days.

_____ 9. May result from brief contact with hot objects.

_____ 10. Only the top layer of skin is damaged.

A. first-degree burns

B. second-degree burns

C. third-degree burns

11. Describe how you should treat a first-degree burn. _____

_____

_____

_____

_____

12. Describe what you would and would *not* do if a child suffered a second-degree burn._____

_____

_____

_____

_____

13. What would you do if a child received a third-degree burn? _____

_____

_____

_____

_____

# Developing Guidance Skills

Direct and Indirect Guidance

Name _____

Date _____ **Period** _____

Read each of the following statements and decide whether direct or indirect guidance is being described. Record your responses on the blank provided.

_____ 1. Removing a hot kettle from the cooking area.

_____ 2. Offering a child choices.

_____ 3. Telling a child what to do.

_____ 4. Lowering the easel so the children can comfortably reach the paper.

_____ 5. Moving a child's coat hook to a lower position in his or her locker.

_____ 6. Saying to a child, "Mary, you need to pick up that paper."

_____ 7. Telling Tom, "You'll lose your turn if you keep pushing."

_____ 8. Adding simple puzzles to the small manipulative area.

_____ 9. Providing a place mat with an outline of a glass, plate, spoon, and fork.

_____ 10. Suggesting to Wendy that she place her arm around Kris, who is crying.

_____ 11. Telling a child that her painting is beautiful.

_____ 12. Keeping your back to the wall so you can observe the entire classroom.

_____ 13. Reminding children to cover their mouths when they cough.

_____ 14. Placing a picture of the toy wagon on the shelf where it is stored.

_____ 15. Purchasing two additional scooters for the playground since the scooter is a popular choice during free play.

_____ 16. Encouraging the children to work together by saying, "Ask Eve if she can help you."

_____ 17. Recognizing a child's accomplishment by saying, "I like the way you helped Amy."

_____ 18. Providing training scissors in the art area so Amanda can learn to cut.

_____ 19. Showing approval by smiling at Jamal after he finished a puzzle.

_____ 20. Seating Ethan and Chris apart during story time to prevent arguments.

Positive Guidance

Name _____

Date _____ Period_____

Children are more likely to respond to positive statements than negative ones. Rewrite each statement below so it tells the child what he or she is expected to do.

1. "Don't put the scissors on the floor."_____

_____

2. "Quit yelling."_____

_____

3. "Don't spill your milk."_____

_____

4. "Don't walk in front of the slide."_____

_____

5. "You'll get water on your clothes."_____

_____

6. "Don't spill sand."_____

_____

7. "You're pouring too fast."_____

_____

8. "Don't get the book dirty."_____

_____

9. "Don't walk so slow."_____

_____

10. "Don't touch all the muffins."_____

_____

11. "Don't ride on the grass."_____

_____

12. "You're hurting the bunny."_____

_____

13. "Get off the gym."_____

_____

14. "Don't eat the macaroni with your fingers."_____

_____

Putting Effective Guidance into Practice

Activity C

Chapter 14

Name _____

Date _____ Period _____

For each of the guidance techniques listed below, describe a situation where it would be appropriate to use. Then describe what you would do and say in each situation. Include all dialogue.

Positive Reinforcement

Describe the situation. _____

_____

_____

Describe how you would use positive reinforcement. _____

_____

_____

Natural Consequences

Describe the situation. _____

_____

_____

Describe how you would use natural consequences. _____

_____

_____

Logical Consequences

Describe the situation. _____

_____

_____

Describe how you would use logical consequences. _____

_____

_____

I-Message

Describe the situation. _____

_____

_____

Describe how you would use an I-message. _____

_____

_____

Promoting a Positive Self-Concept

Describe the situation. _____

_____

_____

Describe how you would use this situation to promote the child's self-concept. _____

_____

_____

Guidance Techniques

Name _____

Date _____ Period_____

Match each of the following statements to the letter of the guidance technique it illustrates. Then write an example of your own for each guidance technique listed.

_____ 1. "Sharon, paint only on your own paper. If you paint on Sandra's paper again, you'll have to move."

_____ 2. "Sally, let's draw on the chalkboard instead."

_____ 3. "Sue, what are the rules for using the jungle gym?"

_____ 4. "I liked the way you helped Kelsie."

_____ 5. "Wendy is having a temper tantrum. Pay no attention to her."

_____ 6. "Tommy, here is a paper towel."

_____ 7. "Peggy, I'm sorry. Here is a glass of juice."

_____ 8. "Lucia, I know you can do it!"

_____ 9. John said, "Steve won't give me play dough." The teacher repeated the statement. Then she added, "You're angry because Steve will not give you play dough."

_____ 10. "Use this pair of scissors. It does not have glue on its cutting edge, so it will cut easier."

A. ignoring

B. active listening

C. modeling

D. persuading

E. praising

F. prompting

G. encouraging

H. redirecting

I. suggesting

J. warning

1. _____

_____

2. _____

_____

3. _____

_____

4. _____

_____

5. _____

_____

6. _____

_____

7. _____

_____

8. _____

_____

9. _____

_____

10. _____

_____

Establishing Classroom Limits

Stating the Positive

Name _____

Date _____ Period_____

Limits should be stated in a language the children can understand. They should also be simple, short, and positive. Limits should always give the children direction. State the following limits positively, telling the children what to do.

Example limit	Limit rewritten in positive form
1. Don't stand on the slide.	
2. Don't just leave what you've spilled.	
3. Don't leave the puzzle on the floor.	
4. Don't tear the pages of the book.	
5. Don't run in the classroom.	

Limit Pyramid

Name _____

Date _____ Period_____

Fill the pyramid with the words that are missing from the limits.

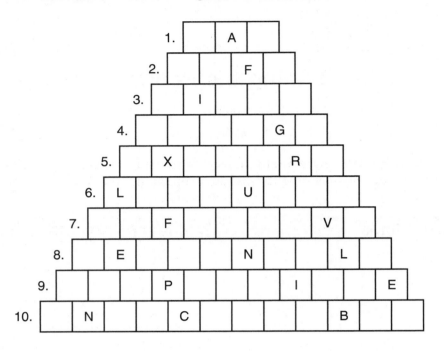

1. According to the _____, children's health and safety must be protected.

2. Limits help make the classroom a _____ place for children.

3. Every _____ should be stated in a specific and positive way.

4. Any _____ in limits should always be discussed with the staff.

5. Children feel freer to _____ when they know their teacher will stop them if they go too far.

6. Limits should be written in a _____ children understand.

7. _____ limits serve as a kind of shorthand that state the goals of the center.

8. Limits that are not _____ can cause young children to feel angry.

9. Teachers are _____ for suggesting new limits to the director and staff.

10. _____ behavior needs to be stopped.

Know the Limits

Name _____

Date _____ Period_____

Circle *T* if the statement is true or *F* if the statement is false.

T F   1. Limits are necessary only on the playground.

T F   2. It is the center director's responsibility to explain and enforce limits.

T F   3. A copy of the limits should be posted on the bulletin board in the teacher's lounge and in the classroom.

T F   4. Limits help children develop self-control.

T F   5. Limits should be stated negatively, in terms of behavior to avoid.

T F   6. Unreasonable limits can cause young children to feel angry.

T F   7. All limits should have a useful function.

T F   8. Limits need to be reexamined on a regular basis by the entire staff.

T F   9. When a limit no longer fits the group's needs, it should be discarded.

T F   10. Unacceptable behavior should be stopped firmly and quickly.

T F   11. Limits need to be inflexible.

T F   12. Depending on the material being used for sensory play, limits may change somewhat.

T F   13. Children must wash their hands before participating in a cooking activity.

T F   14. Limits in the art area are usually minimal.

T F   15. Teachers need to demonstrate some of the limits in the science area.

Describe what you think might happen if a center did not have limits. _____

_____

_____

_____

_____

_____

_____

_____

_____

_____

_____

_____

_____

_____

Setting Limits

Name _____

Date _____ Period_____

Each of the areas in a center needs limits. Think of eight limits a center might have in addition to the limits discussed in the text and list them in the space provided. Indicate the area of the center to which each limit relates.

1. _____
_____

2. _____
_____

3. _____
_____

4. _____
_____

5. _____
_____

6. _____
_____

7. _____
_____

8. _____
_____

Visit a center and list five of its most important limits.

1. _____
_____

2. _____
_____

3. _____
_____

4. _____
_____

5. _____
_____

How do the limits of the center compare with your limits and the limits discussed in the text? _____
_____
_____
_____

Handling Daily Routines

Your Style of Managing Daily Routines

Activity A

Chapter 17

Name _____

Date _____ Period_____

Indicate whether you agree or disagree with the following statements about daily routines. Explain your answers in the space provided.

Agree   **Disagree**

_____ _____   1. Children benefit from following a daily schedule.

_____

_____

_____

_____ _____   2. Children gain satisfaction by doing things for themselves.

_____

_____

_____

_____ _____   3. Teachers should always assist children.

_____

_____

_____

_____ _____   4. Teachers should plan an activity during the arrival time to make the separation from parents easier.

_____

_____

_____

_____ _____   5. Children should be responsible for hanging up their own coats.

_____

_____

_____

_____ _____   6. Demonstrating at the child's eye level is the most effective.

_____

_____

_____

(Continued)

_____ _____ 7. Children should be required to tie their own shoes by age three.

_____

_____

_____

_____ _____ 8. All children must nap.

_____

_____

_____

_____ _____ 9. Four-year-old children should assist in setting the lunch table.

_____

_____

_____

_____ _____ 10. Children should be reprimanded when they spill milk.

_____

_____

_____

_____ _____ 11. Children should be served only one tablespoon of food for each year of age.

_____

_____

_____

_____ _____ 12. Snacks should be provided between meals for children who refuse to eat breakfast.

_____

_____

_____

_____ _____ 13. A dawdling child should be threatened.

_____

_____

_____

_____ _____ 14. Repeated vomiting should be ignored if you are sure the child is not ill.

_____

_____

_____

_____ _____ 15. Toilet learning should be required of children attending a preschool program.

_____

_____

_____

Planning a Daily Schedule

Name _____

Date _____ Period _____

Working in a small group, plan a daily schedule for an early childhood program. Complete the form below as you develop your plans.

Group members: _____

Name of your child care center: _____

Age group and type of program you are offering (all-day, half-day, two-hour): _____

_____

General program goals: _____

_____

Fill in the schedule below, giving times, activities, procedures, and rationale for each time segment.

Daily Schedule			
Time	**Activity**	**Procedures**	**Rationale**

Managing Conflicts

Name _____

Date _____ Period _____

Read each of the following situations. Then work in small groups to discuss them. Write a suggestion for solving each of the conflicts in a positive way.

1. Four-year-old Shyrell refuses to take off her coat. When she arrived at school, she went directly to the art area, picked up a paintbrush, and began to paint. How could you handle this situation?

   _____

   _____

   _____

   _____

2. Luis had a birthday last week. He is now four years old. He still depends on the teacher to help him put on his outdoor clothing. Will this cause Luis to become more dependent or more independent? What advice do you have for the teacher?

   _____

   _____

   _____

   _____

3. Blanca does not appear to have an interest in food. Every day her teacher reminds her to eat during mealtime. Blanca does not seem to take the teacher's advice. Sometimes the teacher even tries to feed Blanca, but this does not appear to be effective. What advice do you have for Blanca's teacher?

   _____

   _____

   _____

   _____

4. All children are expected to remain at the table until everyone is finished eating. However, Andi usually leaves the table before her peers have finished. So far her teacher has been ignoring this behavior. How may Andi's behavior affect the other children? What actions should Andi's teacher take?

   _____

   _____

   _____

   _____

5. After lying down on their cots at nap time, Rivka and Kato ask for a drink of water. This happens every day. Many times after they get water, the other children also request it. How can you prevent this from happening?

   _____

   _____

   _____

   _____

A Sample Lesson

Activity E

Chapter 18

Name _____

Date _____ Period _____

Write a sample lesson plan for a group activity of your choice. Fill in the information requested in the space provided and share your plan with others in class.

Date: _____ Time: _____

Group: _____

Activity: _____

Goals: _____

_____

_____

_____

_____

_____

_____

_____

Learning objectives: _____

_____

_____

_____

_____

Materials needed: _____

_____

_____

_____

_____

Motivation/introduction: _____

_____

_____

_____

_____

_____

(Continued)

Procedures: _____

_____

_____

_____

_____

_____

_____

_____

Closure/transition: _____

_____

_____

_____

Evaluation: _____

_____

_____

_____

_____

_____

_____

Guiding Play and Puppetry Experiences

Playtime Match

Name _____

Date _____ Period_____

Match the following terms and definitions by placing the correct letters in the corresponding blanks.

_____ 1. Commenting to children who follow desired behavior.

_____ 2. Contains materials and equipment that encourages children to explore roles.

_____ 3. Form of social play in which several children play together as they imitate others.

_____ 4. The third stage of material use in play that occurs when children do not need realistic props to play.

_____ 5. Play between two or more children.

_____ 6. Children play by themselves, but stay close to other children.

_____ 7. Occurs when the teacher shows the correct behavior for children during their socio-dramatic play.

_____ 8. Form of play in which a child imitates others.

_____ 9. Giving human traits to nonliving objects.

_____ 10. Two or more forces that oppose each other.

_____ 11. Skill that requires the teacher to provide children with ideas for difficult situations.

_____ 12. Type of play that allows a child to imitate others while using puppets in play.

_____ 13. The second stage of material use that occurs when children use props as intended while playing with other children.

_____ 14. Form of play in which children play alone without involving other children.

_____ 15. Occurs when a child displaces his or her emotions onto an object.

_____ 16. Type of play in which children mimic various adult roles.

_____ 17. The first stage of material use that occurs when children handle the props they are given.

_____ 18. Figure designed in likeness to an animal or human.

A. prop box
B. coaching
C. conflict
D. cooperative play
E. dramatic play
F. reinforcing
G. functional stage
H. imaginative stage
I. manipulative stage
J. modeling
K. parallel play
L. personification
M. projection
N. puppet
O. puppetry
P. role-playing
Q. socio-dramatic play
R. solitary play

Encouraging Socio-Dramatic Play

Name _____

Date _____ Period_____

Prop boxes are used to extend children's play. In the space below, list materials that could be included in a prop box for an office worker, painter, baker, and carpenter. Think of two other categories and list the materials that could be included in a prop box for each of those categories.

Office Worker	Painter
Baker	**Carpenter**

Describe several actions a teacher could take to encourage children to participate in socio-dramatic play.

_____

_____

_____

_____

_____

_____

_____

_____

_____

_____

_____

_____

_____

_____

_____

Design a Puppet

Name _____

Date _____ Period_____

Design a puppet for use with preschool children. Answer the questions below.

1. What type of puppet are you designing? (hand, mascot, "me") _____

2. What is your puppet's name? _____

3. Sketch your design for the puppet:

4. List the materials you will need to create the puppet:

_____ _____

_____ _____

_____ _____

_____ _____

_____ _____

_____ _____

5. In what area of the curriculum could this puppet be used? _____

Give specific examples for its use: _____

_____

_____

(Continued)

6. How could your puppet be used to learn more about what an individual child is thinking or feeling? _____

_____

_____

_____

7. Optional: If you are able to use your puppet with preschoolers, tell about your experience. How did you use the puppet? How did the children react to your puppet? _____

_____

_____

_____

_____

_____

_____

_____

_____

Writing Puppet Stories

Name _____

Date _____ Period _____

Reread the information on puppets in the chapter. Then write a puppet story. Begin with a theme and develop a plot. Use the space below to write the story.

Theme: _____

_____

_____

_____

Story: _____

_____

_____

_____

_____

_____

_____

_____

_____

_____

_____

_____

_____

_____

_____

_____

_____

_____

_____

_____

_____

_____

_____

_____

(Continued)

Methods of Teaching Science

Name _____

Date _____ Period_____

You can use many objects, ideas, and events that are familiar to children to teach them science concepts. Listed below are the methods that were discussed in the chapter. List at least three science concepts that children could learn through each method of teaching.

1. Using color to teach science: _____

   _____

   _____

   _____

   _____

2. Using water to teach science: _____

   _____

   _____

   _____

   _____

3. Using foods to teach science: _____

   _____

   _____

   _____

   _____

4. Using the child's own body to teach science: _____

   _____

   _____

   _____

   _____

5. Using gardening to teach science: _____

   _____

   _____

   _____

   _____

6. Using air to teach science: _____

   _____

   _____

   _____

   _____

(Continued)

7. Using magnets to teach science: _____

_____

_____

_____

_____

8. Using wheels to teach science: _____

_____

_____

_____

_____

9. Using field trips to teach science: _____

_____

_____

_____

_____

10. Using animals to teach science: _____

_____

_____

_____

_____

Guiding Food and Nutrition Experiences

Teaching Nutrition

Name _____

Date _____ Period _____

Develop a colorful rebus chart that presents basic nutrition information. In a *rebus chart*, basic drawings, symbols, or pictures are used in place of the words they represent. For example, the drawing 👁 might replace the word *I*. Then describe how you would use this chart to explain the concepts to a group of young children.

How could you use this chart to explain nutrition concepts to a group of young children? _____

_____

_____

_____

Collecting Recipes

Name _____

Date _____ Period _____

Research cookbooks and find two nutritious recipes that could be used with children. Write the recipes on the recipe cards provided. Beneath each recipe card, develop a recipe chart. Number each step on the chart and use very simple descriptions of the steps. Design the chart so young children will be able to follow along with your help.

Recipe: _____

Recipe Chart

(Continued)

Recipe: _____

Recipe Chart

Setting the Table

Name _____

Date _____ Period_____

Design a place mat for teaching children how to set the table. Include a plate, glass, fork, spoon, and napkin. Draw your place mat in the space provided. You can turn the page horizontally if you wish.

 **Guiding Music and Movement Experiences**

Musical Truths

Read the following statements about music. Circle *T* if the statement is true or *F* if the statement is false.

T   F   1. Music is a form of communication.

T   F   2. Music helps build community.

T   F   3. Music can be used to teach children language skills.

T   F   4. Music experiences can help children build positive self-concepts.

T   F   5. The music area should be located in a small corner of the classroom.

T   F   6. Music experiences should always be structured.

T   F   7. Teachers need to have loud singing voices.

T   F   8. Children respond better to spoken directions than to musical directions.

T   F   9. Music activities should be set in a time and place.

T   F   10. The best songs for young children have a strongly defined mood or rhythm.

T   F   11. Adding new words to a known melody is an easy way to make a song.

T   F   12. The whole song method is best for teaching long songs.

T   F   13. The teacher's enthusiasm and enjoyment of music are more important than a polished musical performance.

T   F   14. The Autoharp® has several advantages over a piano.

T   F   15. The guitar is easier to play than the Autoharp®.

T   F   16. Rhythm instruments can be used to accompany the beat of a recording.

T   F   17. If possible, use seven or eight types of rhythm instruments at one time.

T   F   18. Children of all ages can enjoy sandpaper blocks.

T   F   19. The children can take part in making rattlers.

T   F   20. Children need to be taught how to listen.

T   F   21. Children learn to explore and express their imaginations during movement activities.

T   F   22. Movement activities are most successful when the children are tired and irritable.

Rhythm Instruments

Name _____

Date_____ **Period**_____

Choose one of the rhythm instruments listed below. Develop and perform a demonstration on how to make and use this instrument. Write your notes for the demonstration in the space provided.

sandpaper blocks	rattlers	tin can tom-toms
sandpaper sticks	shakers	coconut cymbals
bongo drums	rhythm sticks	jingle sticks
tom-tom drums	rhythm bells	

Instrument to be used:_____

Notes for demonstration: _____

_____

_____

_____

_____

_____

_____

_____

_____

_____

_____

_____

_____

_____

_____

_____

_____

_____

_____

_____

_____

_____

_____

_____

Fingerplays

Name _____

Date _____ **Period**_____

List two considerations for choosing a fingerplay for a two-year-old.

1. _____

2. _____

In the space provided, write an original fingerplay that you could teach to a two-year-old child. Include descriptions of the actions that go along with the words.

_____

_____

_____

_____

_____

_____

_____

_____

_____

_____

_____

_____

_____

_____

_____

_____

_____

_____

_____

_____

_____

_____

_____

_____

_____

Teaching Movement

Name _____

Date _____ Period_____

Resolve each situation below by providing an appropriate solution.

1. You are going to teach children to clap with their hands. How can you do this?

   _____

   _____

   _____

2. You are assigned to teach a movement activity. How can you prepare for this?

   _____

   _____

   _____

3. One of the first movement activities should focus on listening. What type of beat should you provide for two-year-olds?

   _____

   _____

   _____

4. Space awareness is part of the preschool curriculum. How can you teach this concept?

   _____

   _____

   _____

5. You have been assigned to teach a word game. What types of words should you use?

   _____

   _____

   _____

6. You are going to teach four- and five-year-old children a moving shape game. What could you have the children do?

   _____

   _____

   _____

7. You are planning a pantomiming activity. For what age level would this activity be most suitable?

   _____

   _____

   _____

Guiding Field Trip Experiences

Community Field Trips

Name _____

Date _____ **Period**_____

List 10 specific field trips in your community that young children would enjoy. List the themes that relate to each trip.

Field Trip	Related Themes
1.	
2.	
3.	
4.	
5.	
6.	
7.	
8.	
9.	
10.	

Planning the Trip

Name _____

Date _____ Period_____

Select one of the field trips from the list you created in Activity A. Fill in the information requested to make plans for the trip. Then trade your plans with another person and offer each other comments and suggestions for improving the plans.

Description of field trip selected:_____

_____

Age of children who will participate: _____

Number of children who will participate: _____

Number of adults who will help:_____

Ways children will learn through participation: _____

_____

_____

_____

_____

Total cost of the trip (including transportation, admission, food, etc.):_____

Time you will leave the center: _____

Approximate time you will return to the center: _____

Your educational goals for the trip:_____

_____

_____

_____

_____

How you will prepare the children for the trip: _____

_____

_____

_____

_____

Follow-up activities to reinforce learning: _____

_____

_____

_____

_____

_____

_____

Before and After the Field Trip

Name _____

Date _____ Period _____

The success of a field trip depends on how well the teacher prepares before the trip and follows up after the trip. Assume that you will be taking a group of children on a trip to the local post office. Brainstorm a list of specific pretrip preparations. Include plans you will make and information and questions to discuss with the tour guide prior to the field trip. Then brainstorm a list of follow-up activities to help children clarify their learning. Share your lists with others in the class.

Pretrip Preparations	Follow-Up Activities

Completing the Trip

Name _____

Date _____ Period_____

Complete the following statements about field trips by filling in the blanks with the correct words.

community	directions	machinery	resource	tissues
concepts	fall	observation	security	value
concrete	familiar	permission	short	
crowds	file	preparation	social	
curriculum	follow-up	pretrip	theme	

_____ 1. Field trips are an important part of the _____ for preschool children.

_____ 2. Field trips help children develop _____ skills.

_____ 3. Vague _____ become clearer to children as they gain new information.

_____ 4. By participating in field trips children learn about their _____.

_____ 5. Taking field trips helps children practice following _____.

_____ 6. A field trip to the farm may be chosen while children are studying about farms, food, or _____.

_____ 7. A trip to a pumpkin patch or apple orchard can be taken during the _____ season.

_____ 8. The first trips children take should be _____ and nonthreatening.

_____ 9. After taking trips around the neighborhood, field trips may be taken to _____ places.

_____ 10. _____ walks provide a chance to sharpen children's observation skills.

_____ 11. People walks can teach many _____ concepts.

_____ 12. You should keep a _____ on field trips.

_____ 13. The success of a trip depends on your _____.

_____ 14. You should take paper _____ and a first aid kit on the trip.

_____ 15. _____ slips must be signed by parents.

_____ 16. _____ may overwhelm some children.

_____ 17. Guests or field trip hosts are called _____ people.

_____ 18. After setting goals for the trip, always take a _____ if you have never been to the trip site.

_____ 19. To help children clarify what they have learned, plan _____ activities.

_____ 20. Follow-up activities will reinforce the _____ of the experience.

_____ 21. Young children need _____ experiences to connect with their community.

_____ 22. The number of adults needed must be determined to provide maximum _____.

Programs for Infants and Toddlers

Caregiver Traits

Name _____

Date _____ Period_____

Check all the traits listed that you feel an infant or toddler caregiver should model. Then go through the list again. This time check the traits you model. Answer the questions on the next page.

Personal Traits	Traits a Caregiver Should Model	Traits I Model	Personal Traits	Traits a Caregiver Should Model	Traits I Model
cheerful			disinterested		
forgetful			patient		
self-confident			friendly		
honest			shy		
cooperative			warm		
self-disciplined			cold		
unconfident			concerned		
curious			dependable		
active			enthusiastic		
nurturing			moody		
smiling			pleasant		
inflexible			helpful		
consistent			respectful		
reliable			predictable		
well-organized			kind		
trustworthy			understanding		
courteous			responsive		
unpredictable			easily distracted		

(Continued)

1. Compare your list of traits caregivers should model with the lists of others in the class. Did you choose the same traits? Why or why not? _____

_____

_____

_____

_____

_____

2. In what general areas are you a model of positive traits? _____

_____

_____

_____

_____

_____

3. In what areas can you improve? What can you do to improve? _____

_____

_____

_____

_____

_____

4. Do you think a parent should model the same traits as a caregiver? Why or why not? _____

_____

_____

_____

_____

_____

Environment Needs

Name _____

Date _____ Period_____

For each of the following questions, select the best answer and write the letter in the blank. Then give an explanation for each answer in the space provided.

_____ 1. The diapering area should be located next to a(n) _____.

A. entrance   B. sink

Reason:_____

_____

_____ 2. In the feeding area, the floor surface should be _____.

A. washable   B. carpeted

Reason:_____

_____

_____ 3. To prevent back strain for adults, _____-high changing surfaces should be used.

A. hip   B. waist

Reason:_____

_____

_____ 4. The sleeping area should be adjacent to the _____ area.

A. feeding   B. diapering

Reason:_____

_____

_____ 5. To create a separate play area for babies who crawl, _____ dividers should be used.

A. low   B. high

Reason:_____

_____

_____ 6. In crowded areas, toddlers are inclined to _____.

A. cry   B. withdraw

Reason:_____

_____

_____ 7. A carpeted floor in the play area will be _____ for crawling children.

A. warmer   B. uncomfortable

Reason:_____

_____

_____

(Continued)

_____   8. The sleeping area usually uses the _____ space.

      A. least   B. most

Reason:_____

_____

_____   9. Infants _____ need a darkened room to sleep.

      A. do   B. do not

Reason:_____

_____

_____   10. With infants and toddlers, routines are _____ time-consuming than with other preschool children.

      A. more   B. less

Reason:_____

_____

_____   11. Toddlers need more _____ spaces than infants do.

      A. closed   B. open

Reason:_____

_____

_____   12. The _____ area for toddlers should be located near the main entrance.

      A. receiving   B. diapering

Reason:_____

_____

_____   13. Toddlers need one-third to _____ of the total classroom space open for play.

      A. one-half   B. three-fourths

Reason:_____

_____

_____   14. Teachers of infants and toddlers usually prefer _____ flooring.

      A. tile   B. carpeted

Reason:_____

_____

_____   15. The outdoor play areas should have a large, _____ area.

      A. paved   B. grassy

Reason:_____

_____

Toys for Development

Name _____

Date _____ Period_____

Clip pictures of toys from magazines or toy catalogs that promote fine-motor, gross-motor, reaching and grasping, and sound activities. Mount the pictures in the appropriate spaces. If pictures are unavailable, sketch the toys.

Fine-Motor	Gross-Motor

Reaching and Grasping	Sound

Child Care Procedures

Name _____

Date _____ Period_____

The following story tells about Jan's first morning as an assistant in a child care center. Jan makes several mistakes. Read the story and find her errors. In the space provided, explain Jan's errors and tell what she should do in the future to avoid repeating the errors.

A New Job for Jan

Monday was Jan's first day assisting at the local early childhood center. She was thrilled to have gotten the job, and she began the day with enthusiasm.

Jan's first task was to greet parents and their children as they arrived in the receiving area. Five-month-old Timmy Henson began to cry as soon as Jan took him from his father. She quickly ran and placed him in a crib so she could greet other children. Surely Timmy would stop crying soon. Jan continued the morning by first reading a story to several children and then helping to supervise a painting activity.

Time was passing quickly, and Jan realized it was time for a diaper check. The infants were all awake except for Maria and Tom. Jan gently woke them. Tom did not need a change, but Maria was wet. Jan placed Maria on the floor and knelt down next to the crib to change her. Maria was crying, so Jan gave her a pacifier that she found on the floor. Maria was soon content.

As Jan was putting the clean diaper on Maria, she was called to help prepare the morning snack. Jan threw the dirty diaper in the garbage and wiped her hands on her pants. She picked up Maria and returned her to the crib to finish her nap.

Jan then went directly to the kitchen area where she began to cut up apples and cheese for the children's snack. She took the snack to the toddlers who were playing in the gross-motor area. Jan was very tired after her busy morning, so she decided to take a break and read a magazine.

What mistakes did Jan make during her first morning on the job? What can she do to avoid making these mistakes in the future? _____

_____

_____

_____

_____

_____

_____

_____

_____

_____

_____

_____

_____

_____

_____

_____

_____

 **Programs for School-Age Children**

Quality School-Age Programs

Name _____

Date _____ Period_____

Read the following statements. Circle *Y* if the statement is characteristic of a quality school-age program. Circle *N* if it is not.

Y   N   1. Tailored to the needs, abilities, and interests of the children served.

Y   N   2. Mixed-age grouping is used to promote positive peer modeling and the development of leadership skills.

Y   N   3. Teachers use time-out to discipline children.

Y   N   4. Schedules are rigid to teach children self-discipline.

Y   N   5. Children are allowed to help plan curriculum and make choices about activities.

Y   N   6. Environments are entirely designed to promote large group activities.

Y   N   7. Activities are designed to encourage the children to think, reason, question, and experiment.

Y   N   8. Activities foster a sense of dependence.

Y   N   9. Most adult-child interaction takes the form of instruction and verbal directions.

Y   N   10. Staff seek meaningful conversations with children.

Y   N   11. Staff recognize a child's efforts as well as accomplishments.

Y   N   12. A child's treatment by staff depends on the child's cultural background.

Y   N   13. Staff work with children to set clear limits.

Y   N   14. Motor activities focus on competitive games.

Y   N   15. A variety of materials is available for arts and crafts.

Y   N   16. Activities are designed to promote development.

Y   N   17. The reason for limits and expectations are explained to children.

Y   N   18. Staff include the children in problem-solving situations.

Y   N   19. Outdoor activities are limited to competitive games.

Y   N   20. Staff work in partnership with parents to meet each child's goals.

My Ideal Environment

Name _____

Date _____ Period _____

Pretend you are 10 years old. Your family has arranged for you to attend an after-school program until they can pick you up at 5:30 each weekday evening. Describe your ideal environment for the center where you will be. Include both indoor (interest center, quiet areas, open areas) and outdoor space. Describe each area thoroughly, including floor coverings, wall coverings, furniture, and equipment. Keep in mind that this environment must meet the requirements of a quality school-age program.

Indoor Space

General description of my ideal indoor space:

Interest centers in my ideal center:

Quiet areas in my ideal center:

Open areas in my ideal center:

Outdoor Space

General description of my ideal outdoor space:

Design a Survey

Name _____

Date_____ Period_____

Design a survey to be used with school-age children to assess their interests. This information would be used to plan the curriculum for an after-school program. Begin by choosing a title for your survey. Then include the questions or incomplete sentences that you would use in the survey.

Title: _____

_____

_____

_____

_____

_____

_____

_____

_____

_____

_____

_____

_____

_____

_____

_____

_____

_____

_____

_____

_____

_____

_____

_____

_____

_____

_____

_____

_____

_____

_____

_____

Games for Fostering Development

Name _____

Date _____ Period_____

In a small group, brainstorm a list of games that school-age children would enjoy and that would also foster development: physical, cognitive, emotional, or social. List the games under one of the four categories shown below: board, ball, indoor, or outdoor games. Then indicate the type of development each would foster.

Board Games	
Name	**Type of Development**

Outdoor Games	
Name	**Type of Development**

Ball Games	
Name	**Type of Development**

Indoor Games	
Name	**Type of Development**

Guiding Children with Special Needs

Special Needs Match

Activity A

Chapter 31

Name _____

Date _____ Period_____

Match the following terms and definitions.

_____ 1. Is illustrated when a speaker uses a variety of pitches and loudness levels during routine conversation.

_____ 2. An illness that persists over a period of time.

_____ 3. A program plan designed for each child with special needs.

_____ 4. A severe hearing loss that causes a child to have little understandable speech.

_____ 5. Related to the amount of energy or volume used when speaking.

_____ 6. Chemicals or drugs injected into the body.

_____ 7. An artificial limb.

_____ 8. Things that contact the body through touch.

_____ 9. Term used for placing children with special needs in a regular classroom.

_____ 10. Type of epileptic seizure that causes a child to lose consciousness and jerk, thrash, or become stiff.

_____ 11. Technique that involves taking a child's mispronounced words and correctly using them in sentences.

_____ 12. The lowness or highness of the voice.

_____ 13. Having a physical disability but being able to move from place to place.

_____ 14. Food, drugs, or anything taken through the mouth.

_____ 15. Process in which a child who is gifted is assigned to a class with older children.

_____ 16. Process in which the range of experiences is broadened to provide the child with a special curriculum.

_____ 17. Type of epileptic seizure that may go unnoticed.

_____ 18. Airborne substances that are inhaled.

_____ 19. Exceptional skill in one of the following areas: creative or productive thinking, general intellectual ability, psychomotor ability, leadership ability, specific academic aptitudes, visual or performing arts.

A. acceleration

B. ambulatory

C. chronic health need

D. contactants

E. enrichment

F. expansion

G. giftedness

H. grand mal seizure

I. inclusion

J. Individualized Education Plan (IEP)

K. ingestants

L. inhalants

M. injectables

N. loudness

O. petit mal seizure

P. pitch

Q. profound hearing loss

R. prosthesis

S. voice flexibility

Special Communication Needs

Name _____

Date _____ Period_____

To reinforce your understanding of the communication problems children with special needs may have, answer the following questions.

1. How can you identify a child who is hearing impaired? _____

_____

_____

_____

2. What treatment is often used for children who are hearing impaired? _____

_____

_____

_____

3. What are some suggestions for teaching children who are hearing impaired? _____

_____

_____

_____

_____

4. What are articulation problems? _____

_____

_____

5. How can a teacher help children who have articulation problems?_____

_____

_____

_____

6. What can a teacher do to create good speaking conditions for children who stutter? _____

_____

_____

_____

7. What is amblyopia? _____

_____

_____

_____

8. How is amblyopia treated? _____

_____

_____

(Continued)

9. What is glaucoma? _____

_____

_____

_____

_____

10. How is glaucoma treated? _____

_____

_____

_____

11. What is the difference between nearsightedness and farsightedness? _____

_____

_____

_____

_____

12. Explain color deficiency. _____

_____

_____

_____

13. List at least three ways a teacher can help children who have visual disabilities. _____

_____

_____

_____

Physical and Health Disorders

Name _____

Date _____ Period _____

Explain each of the following disorders and describe problems that a child with each disorder would face.

Allergies	
Amputation	
Arthritis	
Asthma	
Autism	
Cerebral palsy	
Cystic fibrosis	
Diabetes	
Down syndrome	
Epilepsy	
Hemophilia	
Leukemia	
Muscular dystrophy	
Spina bifida	

Helping Children Who Have Special Needs

Activity D

Chapter 31

Name _____

Date _____ Period _____

Read a magazine or newspaper article that relates to teaching children with special needs in an inclusionary classroom. Write a report in the space provided. Then summarize what you feel are the most important considerations for teachers and what you learned from the article. Share this information orally with the class.

Title of article: _____

Source of article: _____

Report: _____

Summary comments (important considerations for teachers of children with special needs and what you learned from reading the article): _____

_____

_____

_____

_____

_____

_____

_____

_____

_____

_____

_____

_____

_____

_____

_____

_____

_____

_____

_____

_____

_____

_____

_____

_____

_____

_____

The Child Who Is Gifted

Name _____

Date _____ Period_____

Interview a parent or teacher of a young child who has been identified as gifted to learn more about how to handle this special need. Ask the following questions.

What is the child's age? _____

In what area(s) is the child gifted? _____

_____

_____

How was the child identified as gifted? _____

_____

_____

What characteristics identify the child as being gifted? _____

_____

_____

_____

What special programs have been made available at home, at school, and in the community to help meet the needs of the child who is gifted? _____

_____

_____

_____

Use the space below for more specific questions and answers related to the child you are studying.

_____

_____

_____

_____

_____

_____

_____

_____

_____

_____

_____

_____

_____

_____

Involving Parents and Families

Getting Family Involved

Name _____

Date _____ Period_____

Complete each of the following sentences using the correct word or words.

active
daily news flash
debating
e-mail
letters

newsletters
orientation
parent involvement
planning
positive

problem-solving file
professional
sunshine call
theme
traveling backpack

_____ 1. A telephone call made by a teacher to a family member to communicate praise and support for the child is referred to as a _____.

_____ 2. Many teachers use _____ to create family newsletters, which lowers mailing costs.

_____ 3. _____ refers to patterns of participation in educational programs by families.

_____ 4. To have a successful parent-teacher conference, you must first spend time _____.

_____ 5. Teachers can send children's favorite items home with one child at a time using a _____.

_____ 6. A letter or newsletter should be written using the _____ voice.

_____ 7. Information on problems families may face can be organized into a _____.

_____ 8. Teachers get the most from family volunteers when they provide a(n) _____ or training session.

_____ 9. The _____ is an everyday written communication for families that contains news about events and occasions at the center.

_____ 10. Letters sent to families often include the _____ of the week.

_____ 11. _____ are written communications that often address only one subject and are put out on an "as needed" basis.

_____ 12. It is best to begin and end the parent-teacher conference with a _____ comment.

_____ 13. A problem that often occurs in group discussions is that groups begin _____ among themselves.

_____ 14. When meeting with families, the teacher should always model _____ behavior.

_____ 15. _____ are written communications that include information concerning a variety of topics and are put out on a regular basis.

Family Letters

Name _____

Date _____ **Period** _____

Assume you are a teacher and have been asked to write the first letter of the year to families. Write a letter in the active voice that includes the following information:

- an introduction of yourself and the other teachers
- classroom goals, limits, and expectations
- an invitation to family members to observe and/or take part in the classroom

_____

_____

_____

_____

_____

_____

_____

_____

_____

_____

_____

_____

_____

_____

_____

_____

_____

_____

_____

_____

_____

_____

_____

_____

_____

_____

_____

_____

_____

Family Discussion Groups

Name _____

Date _____ Period_____

In the chart below, list advantages and disadvantages of using discussion groups for teaching parenting information. Then use the chart to answer the questions that follow. Discuss your answers in class.

Advantages of Discussion Groups	Disadvantages of Discussion Groups

1. What do you think is the strongest argument in favor of using discussion groups?_____

_____

_____

_____

_____

(Continued)

2. Why might some family members dislike discussion groups? _____

_____

_____

_____

_____

_____

_____

3. What do you think is the strongest argument against using discussion groups? Why? _____

_____

_____

_____

_____

_____

_____

_____

Teacher Hotline

Name _____

Date _____ Period_____

Pretend you are an advice columnist who writes a "Teacher Hotline" column for an educational journal. Answer the following letters from teachers about their concerns in working with parents.

Dear Teacher Hotline:

I have difficulty working with family members. For some reason, when I point out the family's weaknesses, they get defensive. What should I do?

Signed,
A Discouraged Teacher

Dear Discouraged Teacher:

_____

_____

_____

_____

_____

_____

_____

Sincerely,
T.H.

Dear Teacher Hotline:

My director has asked me to publish a newsletter. I am afraid to confess that I do not know what to include in the newsletter. What should I do? Help!

Signed,
A Confused Teacher

Dear Confused Teacher:

_____

_____

_____

_____

_____

_____

_____

Sincerely,
T.H.

Dear Teacher Hotline,

Whenever parents visit my classroom, I feel uncomfortable. My pulse increases and I feel nervous. How can I relax?

Signed,
An Uncomfortable Teacher

Dear Uncomfortable Teacher:

_____

_____

_____

_____

_____

_____

_____

Sincerely,
T.H.

Dear Teacher Hotline:

Last Tuesday I began my job as a head teacher in a new center. My director has asked me to write the first family letter. My concern is how to make family letters interesting. Can you help?

Signed,
A Questioning Teacher

Dear Questioning Teacher:

_____

_____

_____

_____

_____

_____

_____

Sincerely,
T.H.

(Continued)

Dear Teacher Hotline:

How important are first impressions? Last week I had my first parent-teacher conference. Without thinking I told a parent that his child was a brat. The father got angry and walked out. Now what do I do?

Signed,
Out of Answers

Dear Out of Answers:

_____
_____
_____
_____
_____
_____

Sincerely,
T.H.

Dear Teacher Hotline:

I am embarrassed that I don't know what to do! On Thursday I had a conference with a timid parent. This mother couldn't even hold eye contact with me. We scheduled a continuation of the conference next week. How can I make the mother feel more comfortable?

Signed,
Embarrassed

Dear Embarrassed:

_____
_____
_____
_____
_____
_____

Sincerely,
T.H.

Dear Teacher Hotline,

The staff at my school are having a difficult time scheduling parent-teacher conferences. We are allowed to use the time from 4 to 5 p.m. for this activity three days a month. What should we do?

Signed,
No Answers

Dear No Answers:

_____
_____
_____
_____
_____
_____

Sincerely,
T.H.

Dear Teacher Hotline:

I am working with a parent who insists that I spank his child. How can I convince this father that spanking isn't successful?

Signed,
Opposed

Dear Opposed:

_____
_____
_____
_____
_____
_____

Sincerely,
T.H.

A Career for You in Early Childhood Education

Assessing Your Abilities

Name _____

Date _____ **Period**_____

Effective early childhood teachers have many abilities in common. To find out how your abilities compare, rate your skills in these areas by checking the appropriate blank for each item.

Strongly Agree **Agree** **Disagree** **Strongly Disagree**

Strongly Agree	Agree	Disagree	Strongly Disagree	
_____	_____	_____	_____	1. Interacts well with children.
_____	_____	_____	_____	2. Interacts well with adults.
_____	_____	_____	_____	3. Demonstrates teamwork skills.
_____	_____	_____	_____	4. Works well as a leader.
_____	_____	_____	_____	5. Communicates well verbally.
_____	_____	_____	_____	6. Communicates well in writing.
_____	_____	_____	_____	7. Has solid computer skills.
_____	_____	_____	_____	8. Listens effectively to others.
_____	_____	_____	_____	9. Understands child development.
_____	_____	_____	_____	10. Comforts, nurtures, and praises children effectively.
_____	_____	_____	_____	11. Effectively meets children's physical care and supervision needs.
_____	_____	_____	_____	12. Follows ethical standards.
_____	_____	_____	_____	13. Plans developmentally appropriate curriculum and themes.
_____	_____	_____	_____	14. Uses positive guidance techniques.
_____	_____	_____	_____	15. Makes sound decisions.
_____	_____	_____	_____	16. Solves problems well.
_____	_____	_____	_____	17. Leads group activities effectively.
_____	_____	_____	_____	18. Observes and assesses behavior objectively.
_____	_____	_____	_____	19. Develops appropriate routines, transitions, and schedules.
_____	_____	_____	_____	20. Plans or serves nutritious meals and snacks.
_____	_____	_____	_____	21. Sets and enforces effective limits for children's behavior.
_____	_____	_____	_____	22. Demonstrates first-aid techniques and emergency procedures.
_____	_____	_____	_____	23. Plans effective activity areas.
_____	_____	_____	_____	24. Selects safe and appropriate toys, software, and playground equipment.

Know How to Job Hunt

Name _____

Date _____ Period_____

Decide whether the following statements about job hunting are true or false. Circle *T* if the statement is true or *F* if the statement is false.

T   F   1. Recent graduates should *not* list lab work or volunteer work in their field of study on a résumé.

T   F   2. The ideal time to ask about vacations is during your interview.

T   F   3. In nearly all interviews, applicants are given the opportunity to ask questions.

T   F   4. A brief thank-you note sent soon after an interview is a basic courtesy that serves as a reminder to those you met.

T   F   5. Sending a thank-you note by e-mail is never appropriate.

T   F   6. Keeping a mental record of each cover letter you send is sufficient.

T   F   7. You should try to state success incidents and accomplishments in your interview.

T   F   8. Asking questions of your supervisor and fellow employees will help you learn more about your job and improve your skills.

T   F   9. Interviewers *cannot* legally ask certain questions because they may be discriminatory.

T   F   10. A résumé is a brief summary of your qualifications, skills, and job experiences.

T   F   11. Networking means developing a group of professional contacts.

T   F   12. The hidden job market involves jobs that are advertised informally through word of mouth.

T   F   13. When employers evaluate a résumé, they look for gaps in employment dates, the amount of space given to earlier jobs, and the emphasis on education.

T   F   14. Newspapers list all job titles related to child care under "child care teacher."

T   F   15. As long as you have sent a résumé in advance, you do *not* need to take a résumé to the interview.

T   F   16. You should be careful *not* to volunteer negative information about former employers or yourself during an interview.

T   F   17. When interviewers ask about your weaknesses, answer as quickly as possible and then change the subject.

T   F   18. Reading newspaper ads once a week is more efficient than reading them every day.

T   F   19. Being involved in professional organizations does little to help in the job search.

T   F   20. Your résumé may serve as your own self-inventory.

T   F   21. A networking letter informs people that you are available for employment.

T   F   22. A thank-you letter is an opportunity to restate your interest in the position.

A Job Application

Name _____

Date _____ Period_____

Complete the following job application form. When you are finished, divide into small groups and evaluate one another's applications.

Community Child Care Center

NAME AND ADDRESS

First Name	Middle Name	Last Name	Social Security No.	Date of Application

PERMANENT MAILING ADDRESS				TELEPHONE NO.
Number and street	City	State	Zip code	(Area) Local Number

Are you over 18 years of age?

JOB INTEREST

Title of position for which you are applying:
Full-Time ☐   Part-Time ☐   Permanent ☐   Temporary ☐   Summer ☐
Are you currently employed?   Yes ☐   No ☐   Date available to start:

EDUCATION AND TRAINING

Name and Address (City & State) of Last Grade School Attended	Dates Attended	Major Studies	Did You Graduate? Yes ☐ No ☐

Name and Address (City & State) of Last High School Attended	Dates Attended	Major Studies	Did You Graduate? Yes ☐ No ☐

Name and Address (City & State) of Business Career or Technical School Attended	Dates Attended	Major Studies	Did You Graduate? Yes ☐ No ☐

COLLEGE LEVEL AND ABOVE (Including Junior & Community Colleges)				
SCHOOL NAME	SCHOOL LOCATION (City & State)	DATE GRADUATED (or Years Attended) Month/Year	TYPE OF DEGREE RECEIVED	MAJOR & MINOR FIELD OF STUDY

Your College Grade Point Average =
A =   Lowest Passing =
Awards or Honors:
Special Skills:
Professional Memberships Related to the Position:

(Continued)

Name _____

EMPLOYMENT RECORD

Please list every employer, including part-time. Begin with your present or most recent employer.					
Date	Name & Address— Employer	1 Position or Occupation 2 Department 3 Name of supervisor	Describe Major Duties	Salary or Wages (Monthly)	Reason for Leaving

From
   Month/Year
To
   Month/Year
		1
		2
		3
				Starting
				$_____
				Final
				$_____	

From
   Month/Year
To
   Month/Year
		1
		2
		3
				Starting
				$_____
				Final
				$_____	

From
   Month/Year
To
   Month/Year
		1
		2
		3
				Starting
				$_____
				Final
				$_____	

From
   Month/Year
To
   Month/Year
		1
		2
		3
				Starting
				$_____
				Final
				$_____	

REFERENCES (do not list relatives)

Name	Address	Phone No.	Occupation	Years Known

ADDITIONAL DATA

Have you ever been convicted of a crime (other than traffic or other minor violations)   Yes ☐   No ☐
that would affect your job performance?
If yes, give nature of offence and other circumstances regarding conviction.

Are you a U.S. citizen?   Yes ☐   No ☐
If "No," do you have an alien registration card or valid U.S. work permit?   Yes ☐   No ☐

Non-English languages you read: _____ speak: _____ write: _____

Other special skills, knowledges and abilities that support your qualifications for the position you are seeking:

PHYSICAL STATUS

Do you have any disabilities that would affect your job performance?   Yes ☐   No ☐
If yes, explain:

In completing, and submitting this application, I understand and agree: That any misstatement of material facts will be sufficient reason for immediate withdrawal of this application or, in the event of employment, be deemed cause for dismissal. That my previous employers may be asked for information concerning my employment, character, ability, and experiences. That no question on this application has been answered in such a manner as to disclose my race, religion, or national origin. That if employed, I may be required to furnish proof of age by birth or baptismal certificate.

Signature _____ Date of Application _____

Balancing Multiple Roles

Name _____

Date _____ **Period**_____

Interview an early childhood professional using the questions listed below. Ask this person how he or she balances multiple roles. Record the person's responses in the space provided.

Professional's Name and Position: _____

1. Please list all the roles you have, including family, work, and community roles. _____

   _____

   _____

   _____

2. Which of your roles is the most demanding on your time? the least? Explain. _____

   _____

   _____

   _____

   _____

3. Do you ever feel stressed trying to meet the demands of all your roles? Explain._____

   _____

   _____

   _____

   _____

4. Which roles do you find conflict the most? Explain._____

   _____

   _____

   _____

   _____

5. When two roles compete for the same time, how do you decide which one takes priority? _____

   _____

   _____

   _____

   _____

(Continued)

6. What time-management strategies do you use to help you reduce role strain? _____

_____

_____

_____

_____

_____

7. What three tips would you offer a new professional for balancing multiple roles? _____

_____

_____

_____

_____

_____

Lesson Plan Form

Name _____

Date _____ **Period**_____

Group: _____

Name of activity: _____

Date scheduled: _____ Time scheduled:_____

Developmental goals: _____

_____

_____

_____

_____

_____

_____

Learning objective:_____

_____

_____

_____

_____

_____

Materials needed:_____

_____

_____

_____

_____

Motivation/introduction: _____

_____

_____

_____

_____

_____

_____

(Continued)

Procedures: _____

_____

_____

_____

_____

_____

_____

_____

Closure/transition: _____

_____

_____

_____

_____

Evaluation:

A. The activity: selection and development _____

_____

_____

_____

_____

_____

B. The children's responses _____

_____

_____

_____

_____

_____

C. Teaching strategies _____

_____

_____

_____

_____

_____

Lesson Plan Form

Name _____

Date _____ **Period** _____

Group: _____

Name of activity: _____

Date scheduled: _____ Time scheduled: _____

Developmental goals: _____

_____

_____

_____

_____

_____

_____

_____

Learning objective: _____

_____

_____

_____

_____

_____

_____

Materials needed: _____

_____

_____

_____

_____

_____

_____

Motivation/introduction: _____

_____

_____

_____

_____

_____

_____

(Continued)

Procedures: _____

_____

_____

_____

_____

_____

_____

_____

Closure/transition: _____

_____

_____

_____

_____

Evaluation:

A. The activity: selection and development _____

_____

_____

_____

_____

_____

B. The children's responses _____

_____

_____

_____

_____

_____

C. Teaching strategies _____

_____

_____

_____

_____

_____

Lesson Plan Form

Name _____

Date _____ **Period** _____

Group: _____

Name of activity: _____

Date scheduled: _____ Time scheduled: _____

Developmental goals: _____

_____

_____

_____

_____

_____

_____

_____

Learning objective: _____

_____

_____

_____

_____

_____

_____

Materials needed: _____

_____

_____

_____

_____

_____

_____

Motivation/introduction: _____

_____

_____

_____

_____

_____

_____

(Continued)

Procedures: _____

_____

_____

_____

_____

_____

_____

Closure/transition: _____

_____

_____

_____

_____

Evaluation:

A. The activity: selection and development _____

_____

_____

_____

_____

_____

B. The children's responses _____

_____

_____

_____

_____

C. Teaching strategies _____

_____

_____

_____

_____

_____

Lesson Plan Form

Name _____

Date _____ **Period** _____

Group: _____

Name of activity: _____

Date scheduled: _____ Time scheduled: _____

Developmental goals: _____

_____

_____

_____

_____

_____

_____

Learning objective: _____

_____

_____

_____

_____

_____

_____

Materials needed: _____

_____

_____

_____

_____

_____

Motivation/introduction: _____

_____

_____

_____

_____

_____

_____

(Continued)

Procedures: _____

_____

_____

_____

_____

_____

_____

Closure/transition: _____

_____

_____

_____

_____

Evaluation:

A. The activity: selection and development _____

_____

_____

_____

_____

_____

B. The children's responses _____

_____

_____

_____

_____

C. Teaching strategies _____

_____

_____

_____

_____

_____

Lesson Plan Form

Name _____

Date _____ **Period** _____

Group: _____

Name of activity: _____

Date scheduled: _____ Time scheduled: _____

Developmental goals: _____

_____

_____

_____

_____

_____

_____

_____

Learning objective: _____

_____

_____

_____

_____

_____

Materials needed: _____

_____

_____

_____

_____

_____

_____

Motivation/introduction: _____

_____

_____

_____

_____

_____

_____

(Continued)

Procedures: _____

_____

_____

_____

_____

_____

_____

_____

Closure/transition: _____

_____

_____

_____

_____

Evaluation:

A. The activity: selection and development _____

_____

_____

_____

_____

_____

B. The children's responses _____

_____

_____

_____

_____

C. Teaching strategies _____

_____

_____

_____

_____

_____